797,885 Books
are available to read at

Forgotten Books

www.ForgottenBooks.com

Forgotten Books' App
Available for mobile, tablet & eReader

ISBN 978-1-331-64410-1
PIBN 10217103

This book is a reproduction of an important historical work. Forgotten Books uses state-of-the-art technology to digitally reconstruct the work, preserving the original format whilst repairing imperfections present in the aged copy. In rare cases, an imperfection in the original, such as a blemish or missing page, may be replicated in our edition. We do, however, repair the vast majority of imperfections successfully; any imperfections that remain are intentionally left to preserve the state of such historical works.

Forgotten Books is a registered trademark of FB &c Ltd.
Copyright © 2015 FB &c Ltd.
FB &c Ltd, Dalton House, 60 Windsor Avenue, London, SW19 2RR.
Company number 08720141. Registered in England and Wales.

For support please visit www.forgottenbooks.com

1 MONTH OF FREE READING

at

www.ForgottenBooks.com

By purchasing this book you are eligible for one month membership to ForgottenBooks.com, giving you unlimited access to our entire collection of over 700,000 titles via our web site and mobile apps.

To claim your free month visit: www.forgottenbooks.com/free217103

* Offer is valid for 45 days from date of purchase. Terms and conditions apply.

Similar Books Are Available from
www.forgottenbooks.com

Impromptu Speeches
How to Make Them, by Grenville Kleiser

Thaumaturgia
Or Elucidations of the Marvellous, by Oxonian

Essays on Books
by William Lyon Phelps

The Art of Writing Speaking the English Language
by Sherwin Cody

Bacon's Essays and Wisdom of the Ancients
by Francis Bacon

An Essay Concerning Human Understanding, Vol. 1 of 2
by John Locke

Eighteenth Century Essays on Shakespeare
by David Nichol Smith

An Essay on Anger
by John Fawcett

Helpful Hints on Writing and Reading
by Grenville Kleiser

Appearance and Reality
A Metaphysical Essay, by F. H. Bradley

Character and Heroism
by Ralph Waldo Emerson

Abraham Lincoln
An Essay, by Carl Schurz

Christian Mysticism and Other Essays
by Harry Leroy Haywood

The Ephebic Oath
And Other Essays Other, by Alexander George McAdie

An Essay on the Beautiful
by Plotinus

Essays and Letters
by Leo Tolstoy

Great Pedagogical Essays, Plato to Spencer
by F. V. N. Painter

Essays and Other Writings
by Henry David Thoreau

Essays on Physiognomy
Designed to Promote the Knowledge and the Love of Mankind, by Johann Caspar Lavater

Essays the Superman
by Aurobindo Ghose Sri

TO

WALTER BLAIKIE

KIND FRIEND AND
HELPER

The Author desires to acknowledge the kind permission to reprint these articles, granted by the Editor of the "National Review" (Nos. 1, 2, 3, 5, 6, 8, 9, 10), the Editor of the "Cornhill Magazine" (No. 7), and the Editor of the "Atlantic Monthly" (No. 4).

PREFACE

"Those who live in glass houses should not throw stones."—OLD PROVERB.

SOME one somewhere has said that proverbs are the concentrated wisdom of the ages. But even the wisdom of many generations may, in certain cases, be questioned; and the writer ventures to assert that dwellers in glass houses are, by their very residence there, privileged to throw a few stones.

In plainer words: the writer of fiction surely knows more than the mere reader of it, about the merits or defects of a story. To have attempted to write fiction is to know its difficulties; and a realisation of these gives at once more leniency and more severity to criticism. The novelist will always judge technical faults severely; because he knows that it is generally possible to avoid such blemishes by care and skill. But he will always be more merciful than the novel reader in judging faults of conception, knowing, as every writer

Preface

does, that this is a matter over which the writer has very little control. For the reader will often say, "How stupid of Mr. A. to make such a mistake in the end of his book"; or, "Why did Mrs. B. not change that tiresome bit in her book? it spoilt all the rest"; not knowing that Mr. A. or Mrs. B. were quite as fully aware of the weak bits in their work as their readers were; but that they were powerless to change them. This, readers can never be expected to understand.

The novelist has a further excuse for writing about novels — that no one can write of them with the same deep interest. The reader reads each book for its intrinsic interest or value; the novelist reads it as forming part of a literary movement. This is the reason why you may hear the novelist speak of "a poor novel," or even of "a wretched novel," but you will never hear from his lips that hateful phrase "only a novel," because he knows that rightly used the novel is a great form for the expression of great thoughts. The form has, indeed, been more abused than any other, probably from its apparent simplicity; but this is no reason why it should be spoken of with contempt.

Preface

"Your books are so successful I think *I* must begin to write," is a remark constantly made to authors by unliterary people who imagine that the Art of Fiction is mere child's play.

The causes, developments, and tendencies of a literary movement are often more interesting to study than the individual books that embody it. For this reason the author has tried in these articles to treat some of our present day fiction in a synthetic manner, so as to show the cause, development, and tendencies of each group of books. By studying fiction in this way it may be seen how much each writer owes to his predecessors, and admiration of the individual writer is at once increased and diminished by this knowledge. The consideration that no absolutely new ideas can be found in any author, however great he may be, checks undue admiration; it is realised that other men, his predecessors, have been gradually evolving these ideas which in the fulness of time have found this spokesman, and wanting him, would as surely have found another. But along with this realisation of the author's indebtedness to the past, comes a fuller

Preface

understanding of his personal gifts—of that individual note which belongs to each great writer and is his alone, not a legacy from other minds. It is this individual note which makes us imagine that we find new ideas in certain books —where the ideas are really venerably old, only so recast by passing through the medium of a great mind that the old appears the new. This wonderful re-casting process is the very hall-mark of genius; no second-class talent can bring forth the well-worn ideas all bright and burnished, and wearing what seems an entirely new face.

In reading the work of others, questions like these constantly suggest themselves to one who writes, and this twofold interest in books must be the author's excuse for this little essay in criticism.

JANE H. FINDLATER.

TORQUAY, *January* 1904.

CONTENTS

		PAGE
I.	GREAT WAR NOVELS	1
II.	ON RELIGIOUS NOVELS	33
III.	THE SLUM MOVEMENT IN FICTION	65
IV.	THE SCOT OF FICTION	89
V.	O TEMPORA! O MORES!	111
VI.	THE ART OF NARRATION	138
VII.	GEORGE BORROW	155
VIII.	"AS COMPARED WITH EXCELLENCE"	177
IX.	MODERN TRAGEDY	206
X.	"THE OTHER GRACE"	236
XI.	WALT WHITMAN	251

STONES FROM A GLASS HOUSE

GREAT WAR NOVELS

To rouse new, fresh delight, a book (I speak of novels) must be about one of the old perennial interests of the race. Side-issues, however cleverly they may be treated, are only of ephemeral value: there are no new themes worth writing about, and there never will be. The writer who does not wish to land himself in a literary *cul de sac* must just trudge humbly along the old thoroughfares where the pavements are worn and trodden by the feet of other pilgrims now gone before to their Eternal City—that City which no

Stones from a Glass House

by-way ever yet led up to. Life and Love, Death, Religion, Wealth, Want, and War are among the primal topics which have unending, ever-new interest for the world: no culture is needed that a man may consider any one of these subjects. You may be sure he has seen something of one or other of them. And what he has seen he will rejoice to recognise; what he has felt he will thrill to feel again; what he knows nothing of he will wish to have related to him. The author who handles these subjects, even indifferently, is sure of his audience—but to the author who handles them nobly all the centuries attend.

Of these primal topics, War—one of the most primal among them—has been the least written about by the novelists.

Now, this statement may seem at first sight to be entirely false, for half the heroes of fiction are warriors; but this is just where the difference comes in—the

Great War Novels

Warrior and not the War is the subject of these books, which, instead of being the record of some great international struggle where thousands of men played their insignificant parts, are merely the stories of individuals in whose lives war was an episode, or a background.

Books which attain to the rank of classic War Novels, however, always treat of the War as greater than the Man, instead of the Man as being greater than the War; and in them the romantic is never allowed to overweigh the historical interest. The true War Novel is the modern epic; hence its scarcity—epics not being written every day. The whole trend of recent fiction is against the epic style of narration. The present craze for quickly-developed plots, where the interest is kept at boiling-point from the first page, forbids the stately development of subject which marks the great War Novel, and makes its repetitions, marchings, and counter-marchings

Stones from a Glass House

only a weariness to the majority of readers. They will not see that panoramic effects can only be got by painting on a large canvas, and would like to have the events of the Thirty Years' War compressed for them within the trivial limits of that outcome of modernity — "the 6s. novel." Until this taste for essence of events is conquered, we cannot look for anything like a great new War Novel. When a historical subject is fairly grappled, there is too much to say about it for it to be said in few words; to give any idea of the confusions and distractions of a great national crisis, the ordinary novel limit simply does not suffice, and the effort at undue condensation results in thousands of semi-historical books, where war is only employed as an effective background to throw the foreground figures into relief.

Such books, however effective, however stirring, cannot properly be termed War Novels, and any one who compares them

Great War Novels

with the great models will quickly see where the difference lies.

The genuine War Novel is not really about men and women; these play a subordinate part in it; a nation is the hero we follow, a mourning wasted land is the heroine we grieve over; the impersonal assumes personality for us—we hold our breath over the fate of armies, not of individuals.

It may be objected that a clever historian can do this for us, and that history is not the novelist's province. But just as the painter is to the photographer, so is the novelist to the historian. His province is not to detail the facts of scenes and events, but to give an *impression* of these as seen through the medium of his imagination. If this is powerful enough, he will be able to have a dozen different lights upon the war he describes; for he will see it through the eyes of a dozen different imaginary characters; what we want in a

Stones from a Glass House

War Novel is not every detail of each campaign, but the Idea of war, and this only an imaginative writer can give us. We can get details anywhere—the Idea eludes all but the subtlest writers.

Thus you will see that all the ordinary talents of the novelist are required in addition to the faculty I have noted above: that of informing the impersonal with personality, making the fate of the striving nations more to the reader than the fate of any hero or heroine.

It must not be supposed, however, that the heroes of War Novels may be stocks and stones, or their stories wearisome because a larger interest overshadows them; quite the contrary—they must be creatures of extreme vitality to stand the test of the counter-interest. And this has been the weak point of innumerable "historical" romances: the writers have trusted to the thrill of the historical story to carry them through, and have allowed their characters

Great War Novels

to be wooden and tiresome This is the case in the majority of tales founded on the Mutiny or the French Revolution—the characters are sketchy, the writers having trusted too far to the interest of their setting.

But instead of showing how books ought not to have been written—which is but a thankless task—how much more delightful it is to show how they have been written by masters of the craft. It is a pity that we have to go to the literature of other countries for our examples; the epic of English war has yet to be written—in novel form Poland, Russia, and France each have produced a great War Novel, and each writer approaches his subject in an entirely different manner.

To read Sienkiewicz, Tolstoi, and Zola together, is to get a pleasant sense of the eternal freshness of the creative minds; all three are "modern" in the sense of belonging to our generation of authors;

Stones from a Glass House

but while Tolstoi and Zola are also modern in spirit, Sienkiewicz writes with the spirit of the Ancients.

This is the reason why Sienkiewicz's War Novels *With Fire and Sword* and *The Deluge* will never be so popular as Tolstoi's *War and Peace*, or Zola's *La Débacle*.

For the spirit of the Ancients—the epic note—is pre-eminently impersonal, and, therefore, unpopular. The epic writer is a mere narrator whose personality never obtrudes itself upon the reader; he has no desire whatever to air his own griefs or write of his experiences, for what he has to write of are the experiences of the whole world of men, not merely of himself. He must, indeed, lose sight of himself to attain this epic rank, and look with such an impartial eye beyond his own circle, that his range of vision becomes practically illimitable. What he must be able to describe is, not the world as it

Great War Novels

appears to him, *but as he can imagine it appearing to men entirely different from himself* in every thought of their hearts. This is a task for which gigantic imaginative gifts are required. Almost any educated man or woman can write down what they have themselves passed through, and to this fact we owe the hundreds of autobiographical novels which appear every year—the work of clever people it may be, interesting as human documents, yet quite undeserving of the title of "imaginative" work But a wholly different range of talent is required when the author has to leave experience behind his back, and adventure into the unknown of other men's experiences. The presence or absence of the autobiographical element in a book may, indeed, be taken as a pretty fair test of its literary rank.

Now one might quite as well search for the personality of Homer in the Iliad, as for the personality of Sienkiewicz in *The*

Stones from a Glass House

Deluge and *With Fire and Sword*. This lack of the personal element will always be resented by the modern reader; but there is another and more powerful reason for the unpopularity of Sienkiewicz when compared with Tolstoi and Zola—he has not the emotion of the one nor the realism of the other.

The emotional description of war is what most readers want when they decide to read about it at all. They would like to know "what it feels like" to fight, whether the near presence of death appals even brave men, and so on—and all this Tolstoi can tell them; while yet another class wish to read of more tangible things than emotions. They would like to hear something about the agony of wounds, the convulsions of violent deaths, the horrors of captivity; to such, Zola's ensanguined pages will afford very real enjoyment—here is the realist triumphant,

Great War Novels

up to the elbows in gore, ready with every detail of each dripping campaign!

In this way our authors divide naturally into three distinct schools—the Epic, the Emotional, and the Realistic. I should now like to try to describe their curiously different methods of presentment a little more in detail.

The Epic, as represented by Sienkiewicz, must have the first consideration.

The Deluge—that colossal book—is the history of the Polish wars with Sweden in the seventeenth century. Endless wars—"battles of the warrior with confused noise and garments rolled in blood"—a record this of nameless fights in unknown wildernesses, of struggles, torments, treacheries, and unspeakable valour. "It is written in no book," he says, "how many battles the armies, the nobles, and the people of the Commonwealth fought with the enemy. They fought in forests, in fields, in villages, in hamlets, in towns;

Stones from a Glass House

they fought in Prussia, in Mazovia, in Great Poland, in Little Poland, in Russia, in Lithuania, in Trend; they fought without resting in the day and the night. Every clod of earth was drenched in blood. The names of the knights, their glorious deeds, their great devotion perished from the memory, for the chronicler did not write them down and the lute did not celebrate them!" *The Deluge* chronicles some of them however, and it is an extraordinary tribute to the skill of Sienkiewicz that he has been able to make all these hundreds of nameless fights a matter of absorbing interest to his readers. This, I think, comes from his wonderful faculty of giving a personality to the impersonal.

Poland stands before us as we read, not a mere "country on the map of Europe," but wasted, harried, betrayed; a tragic mother of the gallant sons who rush to death for her sake. We follow

Great War Novels

the story of these long and weary troubles as we might trace the sufferings of a woman dear and unhappy. Sienkiewicz writes of his country's grief with such magnetic sympathy that our one wish as we read is that her woes should be ended. Now the heroes who are (in the story) to work out Poland's salvation, become to us dearly-loved and honoured friends, yet we are so fired with the writer's patriotism that we would rather that every hero in the book found his grave if by the sacrifice Poland were delivered; the cause, in short, matters to us, not the men; they are dear to us just because they are patriots; the interest of the book stands or falls on the country's success or defeat. It must not be supposed that Sienkiewicz fails to create interesting characters; on the contrary, so splendid are his creations, that it is little short of an unkindness to have presented them for the admiration of dwellers in an effete age.

Stones from a Glass House

Kmita, the principal hero, is a compound of blood and bone and fire, a resistless foe, an equally resistless lover—the product of a bygone age, with all its virtues and most of its faults. He is the type of the primitive fighter, untouched by speculations on death or futurity as he faces danger, professing and believing a simple creed; a creature belonging to the unquestioning "age of Faith." See him as he starts on his great exploit:—

"The thought of bursting the gigantic gun delighted him to the bottom of his soul . . . and at times *pure laughter seized him.* As he had himself said, he felt no emotion of fear, no unquiet. It did not even enter his head to what an awful danger he was exposing himself; he went on *as a schoolboy goes to an orchard to make havoc among apples.*"

Or, again, at the siege of Yasna Gora he laughs at the trembling monks:—

Great War Novels

"On a sudden, Kmita stretched out his hand and cried 'See, see, you have an experiment.'

"'Jesus! Mary! Joseph!' cried the young brother at the sight of the coming bomb. The bomb fell on the square that moment, and, snarling and rushing along, began to bound on the pavement, dragging behind a small blue smoke; turned once more, and rolling to the foot of the wall on which they were sitting fell into a pile of wet sand, which it scattered high to the battlement, and, losing its power, remained without motion Luckily, it had fallen with the fuse up; but the sulphur was not quenched, for the smoke rose at once.

"'To the ground! on your faces!' frightened voices began to shout. But Kmita at the same moment sprang to the pile of sand, with a lightning movement of his hand caught the fuse, plucked it, pulled it out, and raising his hand with the burning sulphur, cried· 'Rise up, it is just as if you had pulled the

Stones from a Glass House

teeth out of a dog; it could not kill a fly now.'

"When he had said this, he kicked the bomb. Those present grew numb at the sight of this deed, which surpassed human daring. Kmita *laughed so heartily that his teeth glittered.*"

The book is full of such exploits, all of them carried out in the same spirit of gay bravery. The other warriors in *The Deluge* are of this heroic breed also, and carry out their feats of arms with equal gallantry. None of them ever speculate about eternity, or have introspective moments of any kind whatever. For them, heaven and hell lay, without a shadow of doubt, just beyond the grave, so what was the need of speculating about futurity? Their simple creed, of course, made for bravery (your questioning fighter is not the best), and there is in these soldiers a delicious mixture of savagery and religion. We read of Kmita that, "when in the

Great War Novels

evening he was *repeating his Litany in peace by the blaze of burning villages*, and the screams of the murdered interrupted the tally of his prayers, he began again from the beginning, so as not to burden his soul with the sin of inattention to the service of God." This is the sort of hero we have to do with in these books. It is interesting to contrast such passages with some from Tolstoi, who glories in the introspective man. I shall quote some of his more characteristic passages later.

The Sienkiewicz heroes are equally splendid in love as in war. Wherever our author approaches the tender passion, it is in the purely idyllic fashion; and in a barbarous age, in a savage country, these warriors are very Bayards—the brutalities of modern fiction are unknown in his pages, yet the excessive virility of the characterisation never suffers for a moment from this fact. Sienkiewicz has a tradition of love which he upholds

Stones from a Glass House

unflinchingly—hot as flame and white as snow are these idyllic love stories; a combination not often found in fiction, whatever may be the case in real life.

For books which treat of savage warfare, there is in *The Deluge* and *With Fire and Sword* a marked avoidance of the barbarous realism which the times might seem to suggest. It is not Sienkiewicz's method to gloat on the horrible or the noisome elements in life. What is absolutely necessary to say he says; the unnecessary horror is decently veiled and passed by. To this fact I think his work owes much of the classic note, which is its characteristic. Beauty in one form or another must always be the subject of all the greatest art, and in losing sight of this primary truth how many have erred! You may get powerful work, amusing work, clever work on the lines of ugliness; but the greatest of all is never found divorced from beauty. This principle has

Great War Novels

been grasped by Sienkiewicz from the first page of his books to the last. There may be in them much tale of bloodshed and carnage and torture, but a golden thread runs through and through the dark web—the splendid will and courage of man glorify the whole blood-sodden record, and love is triumphant to the close.

But I am, perhaps, writing at too great length about Sienkiewicz, and must remember how much remains to be said about the other two great authors, his rivals. I have, however, sinned with deliberation, because it seems to me that these books attain to a level of greatness much higher than that attained to by either Tolstoi or Zola There is an all-round sanity in them which is wholly wanting in Zola's terrible depictions of war; and a virility which is missing in Tolstoi's beautiful, mystical presentations. The books are, in fact, unique,

Stones from a Glass House

and opening them for the first time we exclaim—

> " Then felt I like some watcher of the skies
> When a new planet swims into his ken ;
> Or like stout Cortez, when with eagle eyes
> He stared at the Pacific—and all his men
> Looked at each other with a wild surmise,
> Silent, upon a peak in Darien."

We find in Tolstoi the great Emotional exponent of war. *War and Peace* is not so much a description of war as a description of what men feel when engaged in it. Tolstoi has the wonderful faculty of catching and expressing those vague sensations, half thoughts, half emotions, which drift across the mind, and by this system of analysis we are made to enter so entirely into the feelings of every character in the book, that we seem to be identified with each of them for a time. The thoughts of each soldier while he is fighting, or as he lies wounded, or as he dies,

Great War Novels

are faithfully written down for us here, so that we get an impression of a fact that we are apt to forget—the continuousness of thought, even through the most awful moments of life. These random, distracted thoughts of the heart at times of fearful crisis are conveyed with marvellous art—always, the reader thinks, that through the mouthpiece of each character he is on the brink of receiving some answer to the unanswerable questions of life. Facing death—staring at it—surely this soldier will be able to see an inch beyond the veil? When Prince André lies wounded on the field wonderful thoughts visit him as he gazes up into the sky:—

"What peace! what rest!" he thought. "It was not so just now when I was running—we were all running and shouting; it was not so when those two scared creatures were struggling for the ramrod—the clouds were not floating then

Stones from a Glass House

in that infinite space! How is it that I never noticed these infinite depths before? How glad I am to have seen them now—at last. Everything is a hollow delusion excepting that—thank God for this peace, this silent rest!" And, later, when André is carried past Napoleon, he thinks on and on in the same strain: "What, after all, were the interests, pride, elation of Napoleon—what was the hero himself when compared with that glorious heaven of justice and mercy which his soul had felt and apprehended? To him everything seemed sordid, petty; so unlike those stern and solemn thoughts that had been borne in upon him by his utter exhaustion and expectation of death. Even with his eyes fixed on the Emperor he was reflecting *on the insignificance of life, of which no one knew the aim or end—the still greater insignificance of death, whose purpose is inscrutably hidden from the living.*"

This is different indeed from Kmita

Great War Novels

"seized with pure laughter" at the time of his greatest peril! Yet Tolstoi's heroes are no cowards, only introspective men—men of this century, written about by a man perhaps more introspective than themselves. For there is a good deal of the personal note in Tolstoi—his own opinions, not the opinions of his characters, his own sensations, not the sensations of other men, are described for us; and in this way a certain sameness creeps into the story, for the characters have so many sensations and thoughts in common—beautiful as these may be. Every man in the book is speculating, questioning, drifting to and fro on a sea of doubts, and never coming to anchorage; the analysis is really of one mind, not of many as it professes to be. But it is not, after all, with men that Tolstoi is concerned here, so much as with the consideration of war as a phenomenon.

What is this scourge of God that is

Stones from a Glass House

laid so heavily on the bleeding lands? What does it mean? How is it to be accounted for? Tolstoi has very definite views on the subject. We are far too apt, says he, to assign trivial causes for great historical events — we say that certain kings or certain generals brought about certain wars, carried them through successfully or disastrously, and so on. Whereas men had nothing to do with it. Here is Tolstoi's position :—

"To say" (for instance) "that Napoleon sacrificed the army voluntarily or by sheer incapacity is just as false as it is to say that he led his troops to Moscow by the vigour of his will or the brilliancy of his genius. In either case *his personal action had no more influence than that of the meanest private*, it had to bow to certain laws of which the outcome was the resultant fact. . . . The greater the number, the greater the strength, says military science, consequently great battalions

Great War Novels

always win the day. But in defending such a proposition, military science is in the same kind of error as a theory of physics would be which, being based on the relation of force to mass, should regard the first as bearing a direct ratio to the second. But force is the product of the mass multiplied by velocity. And in war the force of the troops is also the product of the mass, *but the multiplier is an unknown quantity*. Military science does vaguely admit the existence of an unknown quantity, and tries to find it in the mathematical precision of the plans adopted, in the mode of arming the men, or *more frequently in the genius of the leader*. But the results attributable to this multiplier still do not agree with the historical facts; to discover this unknown x we have only to give up once for all the hero-worship which leads us to ascribe extravagant importance to the measures taken by Commanders-in-Chief. This x is the spirit of the men; their greater or less eagerness to fight, to face danger—

Stones from a Glass House

it is quite irrespective of the genius of generals. . . ."

But Tolstoi does not take into consideration in this much-reasoned theory the effect which the despised generals may have or may not have upon the all-important spirit of the troops. His theory deepens, however, into a much more mystical stage than this, and he takes up what, after all, is a more reasonable position :—

" The drama at last was ended. The Actor (Napoleon) was bidden to take off his finery, to wipe the paint from his face; he was wanted no more. The Manager of the Great Drama having allowed him to end his part, and stripped the Actor, now displayed him as he really was. 'Look at him, see what you have been believing in all the while! *Now do you not see that it was not he but I that moved the world?*' And still, blinded by the mighty movement, men were long before they understood this."

Great War Novels

You will see from these extracts how entirely different Tolstoi and Sienkiewicz are in their outlook on war. To the one it is a great phenomenon having a mystical source—a sort of writing on the wall of Time which all men may read and see there the helpless littleness of the creature under the great hand of God; while to the other war does not appear as a phenomenon in the least, but as the stirring yet everyday work of those who are called to fight. To Sienkiewicz war involves no problem.

Both of these contentions being quite tenable, it is interesting to find that Zola has constructed a third theory of what war is.

I must leave my readers to judge for themselves which of the three is the most sane and reasonable. No doubt when a dozen other War Novelists have arisen each will bring out another theory, for, said Pilate, "What is truth?"

Stones from a Glass House

If you will have realism, there can be no doubt that *La Débacle* takes a first place as the great realistic War Novel.

As a mere describer Zola stands alone—he can describe anything so as to bring it vividly before the fancy of his readers. This wonderful gift has been brought to bear upon the subject of war, and a remarkable book is the result of it. To name *La Débacle* a novel would be quite absurd; but that it is a War Novel is undoubted. Hero or heroine there is none in the book, for the characters are the merest shadows bearing names; but France is the heroine, a people the hero, their fall and fate the plot, the interest, the whole—the book is steeped in passionate patriotism: more than this, *La Débacle* treats of the whole Idea of war—Zola's idea of it—and as such must be of interest. What this idea is, I shall show later; in the meantime, let me note

Great War Novels

the secret of Zola's popularity as a War Novelist.

It cannot be (in England) his patriotism; there is no plot to interest any one, neither is the characterisation sufficiently clever to attract many readers; any history book will give with equal veracity the story of this campaign; but Zola alone, perhaps, among living writers, could have written of its appearances. The history of a campaign is one thing, and a description of it is quite another. To put it quite plainly, the unvarnished horrors of *La Débacle* account for its popularity.

At first sight one is tempted to exclaim, "What an imagination the man must have!" till, on closer inspection, one sees that the book is only a mass of collected facts curiously untouched by imagination. On the emotional side lies Zola's weakness—too constant and close observation of the mechanical details of outside things has weakened his insight into what lies

Stones from a Glass House

below the surface. In *La Débacle* the exterior of warfare is reproduced with photographic accuracy, but its spirit is entirely missed. This is where the want of sympathetic imagination comes in. No thrilling guess at *what war means to other men* has ever swept through the heart of this man, who is an observer and describer of what he himself notices on the crowded surface of a swarming world—and only that. He describes brilliantly his own idea of war, but cannot imagine any one else having any other idea of it. His position is accurately summed up in the words of one of his characters, who is said to have "a vision of what war really was—an *atrocious* vital struggle, which man should accept only with a grave and resigned heart, as he would some fatal law." This is the idea which Zola carries out all through *La Débacle*, and puts into the mouth of each of his characters Now, to the majority of

Great War Novels

soldiers, war is the most splendid and delightful event in their lives: they see nothing "atrocious" in it, and will even speak of it as the best of fun—there is little or nothing of the "grave and resigned heart" about them. An imaginative author, able to conceive of characters wholly different from himself, must have put some of this spirit into some of his creations, whatever his private views upon the subject might be.

The whole romance of war is absent from this great and terrible book; the iron hand of the realist does not permit of romance. That it is the history of a great catastrophe does not explain this entirely; no troops worthy the name—far less the great, if ill-fated army of France—ever went out to war in the sodden spirit of Zola's soldiers. Such a set of grumbling cravens would never have gone to death as these men did in the tragic fields of Sedan. For men will not die for nothing

Stones from a Glass House

—the great, romantic Spirit of War was there, though Zola does not admit the fact. "The letter killeth — the Spirit giveth life"; *La Débacle* is a brilliant description of "the letter" of War; but the life that should animate the clay is wanting.

Why have we no War Novelist in our literature who can rank along with these three great men, Sienkiewicz, Tolstoi, and Zola? England surely has had wars enough, and writers enough—but the two have not joined, as it were. If Shakespeare had lived nowadays Henry the Fifth would have been a novel, no doubt —but then Shakespeare does not live nowadays. What can we say, then, but "Come, O Breath, and breathe on us" that the great War Novelist may arise!

ON RELIGIOUS NOVELS

A NEW cure for old griefs: the physician who has this to offer will never want for patients.

The readers of religious novels—like those persons who will not try well-known remedies yet are glad to experiment with every newly advertised drug—these readers are ever on the watch for fresh faiths. Oppressed with a thousand sorrows as old as Time, they still crowd forward, with strange optimism, to try the new recipes for joy. I think that here we have the real reason for the extraordinary popularity of "religious" fiction; it is one more cure for the ills of a world which has "ailed from the first." Not an abstract love of truth, not even a deep interest in theology, is at the root of this demand for

Stones from a Glass House

religious fiction—but the intensely personal question, "Will these books help me to be happier?"

There can be no doubt that the majority of mankind like to be led by some guide or other. Independent judgment on any subject is an exceedingly rare thing to meet with; and this is especially the case in matters of religion. We either do not wish to be troubled to decide for ourselves, or, perhaps, we feel an incapacity to do so satisfactorily. Be that as it may, the fact remains that most of us have accepted the views of other people about religion and named them our beliefs. The whole machinery of churches, clergy, priests, is a standing proof of this fact. We want guides, men better qualified than ourselves to deal with the mysteries of religion, to decide for us what we are to believe. There is something pathetic in this universal confession of weakness: we cannot even make our own way straight

On Religious Novels

to our gods: some one must be there to point out the road to us. When once it is recognised that the great majority of people are led, and that only a small minority think for themselves, the question of who the guides are becomes one of great importance. Looking back over "the past's tremendous disarray," we can only wonder and sorrow over the curious credulity of man, who has followed blind guides unquestioningly all the ages through, and is following them still, though not quite so unquestioningly. The tremendous ascendency of the clergy which prevailed in other days is now a thing of the past: they influence still, but they dominate no longer. We may believe their teachings if we wish to, but it is not now a choice between orthodoxy and the stake.

There is, however, a danger of another sort ahead; for as the influence of the clergy has decreased the influence of the Press has increased, so that the dominion

Stones from a Glass House

has only been transferred to fresh hands, instead of being done away with. Thousands—tens of thousands—of people, who in former days would have been staunch Churchmen, repeating their creed like parrots, entirely unquestioning of its truth or falsity, have now as blindly taken their creeds from books of various kinds, from newspapers and popular magazines. Such persons will tell you that they "have ceased to believe in the Church"; but in nine cases out of ten they have taken up their attitude quite unthinkingly, and from stupidity rather than from deep intellectual causes. They have simply read and read again all manner of attacks and criticisms on Churches and clergymen, until they came to accept these criticisms as truth without examining their claims with any seriousness. Thinking, clever men attack the creeds and dogmas, and unthinking, stupid men at once find their whole faith undermined and profess to have lost it.

On Religious Novels

How often we hear it said that "thinking men have stopped going to church"—the fact being that fully more unthinking men have done so, and with far more dangerous results. For the one is in no danger from throwing over what we may call "the church habit"—he will continue to think about God and eternity whether he goes to church or stays out of it; but the other, in renouncing the church habit, very often renounces along with it all but the most fleeting thoughts of holiness, unless he is supplied with some new spiritual influence.

It is here that the true province of the religious novel is found. Strange as it seems, there are many thousands of men and women ready and willing to have revised creeds supplied to them ready-made, complete in red boards, at 6s.! For such persons the religious novel supplies a long-felt want and has the most distinct uses. Better any creed than none at all; and as

Stones from a Glass House

the man who is content to accept his creed at the hand of the first author he reads is manifestly unfit to reason things out for himself, it is very easy to see what a responsibility rests with the new creed-makers. For creed-makers they all wish to be after they have done with being creed-breakers.

The thorough-going religious novel—and by this term I do not mean to describe books of a religious tendency, but those which deal plainly with some definite religious problem—must always conform to one stereotyped form. It must, that is to say, be divided into two parts, the destructive and the constructive. For before the hero, or heroine, attains to a new faith, he or she must have passed through a period of unrest and scepticism; this must be described in the first part of the book, while the second must go on to the construction of the new faith on the ruins of the old, and this must form the other half

On Religious Novels

of the story. Plot and character are apt to be falsified by a stereotyped method of this sort which cannot be avoided; the characters are bound to act up to what is expected of them, and this, in most cases, brings an exasperating improbability into the plot. This limitation of method is the reason why the majority of religious novels have to be relegated to the second rank of literature. When "purpose" comes in too boldly at the door, art is apt to fly out of the window; but, after all, if authors wish to be teachers they probably are not ambitious to be artists, the one province being entirely apart from the other.

But to return to our subject. We have seen that a large class of the community is turning for help just now to religious novels: also that this class is not by any means the most intelligent among us. There are, however, other readers for this sort of fiction whose intelligence must not

Stones from a Glass House

be thus called in question—I mean very young people, and the half-educated class.

The ladder of doubt, which generally leads up to some higher ground than that which it rests upon—has to be painfully climbed by most intelligent young creatures between the ages of fifteen and twenty. Let no one speak lightly of these struggles, as of some childish complaint we have all to pass through; for this growth of the soul is a critical process of far-reaching importance. There is no light acceptance here of the first creed that comes to hand: in a very agony of scepticism the straining young intellect will reject every argument or theory of the Universe which is offered to it by the orthodox, well-known guides. For it is a characteristic of youth that it must always be in a state of revolt from authority when in its period of growth; a necessity seems to be laid upon it to reject every dogma it

On Religious Novels

has been brought up to believe, and to turn to new guides.

The influence of religious novels on such readers is often very profound, and very helpful for a time. Later on they may outgrow these teachers, but in the "present distress" they afford comfort and guidance. They see all their doubts and despairs reflected here, and take courage—others have passed the lions, the House Beautiful may yet be ahead, and the Delectable Mountains may be gained at last. But the benefit of religious fiction to half-educated readers is much more questionable. The book which may comfort the doubter may easily torment the man who has never begun to doubt. He is presented in an easy, readable form with a sort of digest of modern thought, more or less convincingly put. These ideas are hopelessly at variance with the creeds of his childhood, yet time and opportunity both fail

Stones from a Glass House

him to examine into their truth or falsehood. Such are the inevitable and melancholy results of cheap education and cheap culture—one more illustration of the truth that "a little learning is a dangerous thing."

Now to meet this hunger for help and truth and guidance, which is such a real want just now, only a few really good religious novels have ever been written. You might count them on your fingers. The number of indifferently good ones is countless, while of sorry trash there is no end at all. But in making this assertion I would wish you again to remember that I do not write of books of a religious tendency, but of those which deal with some definite dogmatic problem. Let us see what the best of these books have to teach—the others do not concern us.

The doubts of the children are seldom those that perplexed their fathers. It is true that they have each the same scheme

On Religious Novels

of things to puzzle over; but each generation stumbles over some new stone on the old path. The fathers perhaps find their difficulty in predestination. The sons will find theirs in miracles, and the grandsons theirs in the inspiration of Scripture—it is an endless chain. But I think if you examine the principal religious novels, you will find that they have followed, to a great extent, what is the general course of doubt as it rises, grows, and takes possession of the human mind. That is to say, the phases of doubt which succeed each other more or less quickly in the individual, have been slowly worked out during a period of many years by a succession of authors. Let me illustrate my meaning by examples.

What may be termed the first innocent difficulties of most young thinkers about religion rise from an inability to reconcile the justice and omnipotence of God with the origin of evil, or the conception of a

Stones from a Glass House

loving God with the theory of an afterstate of punishment. Now this earliest stage of doubt has its spokesman in George McDonald, one of the pioneers of religious fiction.

The writer (who is not yet grey-headed) can still remember the time when *Robert Falconer* was considered a book of almost atheistic tendency. Yet the doctrines which *Robert Falconer* was written to destroy, are only those of eternal punishment and predestination—old woes of the soul on its heavenward journey, which one seldom hears mentioned nowadays except as a subject of (exceedingly unsuitable) jest. But at the time when *Robert Falconer* was written these doctrines were so universally held that a clever writer like George McDonald thought it worth his while to devote his talents to the task of combating them. He found in these questions an inspiration which he never found again in

On Religious Novels

any of his later, work. "Is God indeed Love?" is the question of questions with George McDonald, and his hero Robert is puzzling over this from the first page to the last. His cry of, "I dinna care for God to love me, gin He doesna love ilka body," has been the cry of most generous young hearts at one time in their experience. Robert, of course, under the care of his stern old Calvinistic grandmother has to pass through the period of revolt—the destructive part of the book has to be set down; but this is so artistically done that the artificiality of the method never appears: we do not think about machinery—we are only interested in the very human difficulties of poor Robert. The second—constructive—half of the book is less convincing, because by this time we begin to perceive the method, and have become aware that it is clearly necessary for Robert, at this point, to begin reconstructing his scheme of things.

Stones from a Glass House

Still, the probability of the story and of the characterisation does not flag—to the last Robert is a real human being to us, not a puppet created to give expression to certain views. And this shows the more admirable skill, because the book is cram full of views—arguments they scarcely deserve to be called. George McDonald takes up the unanswerable ground that religious truths must be felt, and are beyond the reach of proof, and beyond the influence of argument. This position is one too seldom taken up by the polemical novelist of to-day, yet it is, I think, the reason why *Robert Falconer* stands the test of time as it does; "arguments," "proofs," "demonstrations of science," and so forth, are terribly apt to become out of date, or to be overturned by some newer proof or discovery; but the emotional proof is little likely to be superseded. Job's argument is still the best:—"I know that my Redeemer liveth."

On Religious Novels

There is a passage in *Robert Falconer* which exhibits pretty clearly the point that public thought had arrived at at the time the book was written. It is this:—" Robert's mother had taught him to look up—that there was a God. He would put it to the test. Not that he doubted yet; but he doubted whether there was a hearing God. But was not that worse? It was, I think. *For it is of far more consequence what kind of a God, than whether a God at all.*" I doubt if this sentence could have been penned in the Twentieth Century. Since the days of *Robert Falconer* doubt has become far more widely diffused and far more despairing. Thousands in these present evil days would reverse George McDonald's sentence, saying: " It is of far more consequence whether there be a God at all, than of what kind He is"; but this view of things was yet a great way off on the literary horizon.

Stones from a Glass House

The remarkable productions of *Mark Rutherford* seem to me to follow the writings of George McDonald by natural sequence. For they are the evangel of agnosticism, that constant refuge of questioners.

The nightmare quality of *Mark Rutherford* and *Mark Rutherford's Deliverance*, together with the beautiful style in which they are written, single out these books from all other religious novels. They are, in truth, more autobiographies than novels, though they conform strictly to the limitations of the received method for religious fiction; the two books tell, that is to say, of the destruction of Mark Rutherford's faith and of the building up again of something—one can scarcely call it by the cheerful name of faith—by which he lived and died. I have said that these books have a nightmare quality, and the expression is no exaggeration. To use Mark Rutherford's own words, the books

On Religious Novels

tell of "blind wanderings in a world of black fog haunted by apparitions." A sordid, weary world, too—a world of petty tradesmen, who are degraded by their trades and live disgusting, ignoble lives. Rutherford has that fatal type of mind which can never be happy, because he sickens at his own appointed world. He cannot adopt the sensible view that in every class there are fine men who lead honourable lives; he sees nothing but the seamy side of everything. The narrowness of the men he is brought in contact with, instead of amusing him, nearly maddens him, and things go from bad to worse. All this, and Rutherford's decline from orthodox Christianity, are recorded in the *Autobiography;* the *Deliverance* is the sequel to the *Autobiography*. Rutherford has come to the most conclusive of conclusions by this time:—

"No theory of the world is possible.

Stones from a Glass House

The storm, the rain slowly rotting the harvests, children sickening in cellars, are obvious; but equally obvious are an evening in June, the delight of men and women in each other, in music, and in the exercise of thought. There can surely be no question that the sum of satisfaction is increasing . . . as the earth from which we sprang is being worked out of the race, and a higher type is being developed. I may observe, too, that though it is usually supposed, it is erroneously supposed, that it is pure doubt that disturbs or depresses us. Simple suspense is, in fact, very rare, for there are few persons so constituted as to be able to remain in it. It is dogmatism under the cloak of doubt which pulls us down. It is the dogmatism of death, for instance, which we have to avoid. The open grave is dogmatic, and we say, 'That man is gone'—but it is as much a transgression of the limits of certitude as if we were to say, 'He is an angel in bliss.' The proper attitude, the attitude enjoined by the severest exercise

On Religious Novels

of reason, is, '*I do not know*'; and in this there is an element of hope, now rising, now falling, but always sufficient to prevent that feeling of blank despair which we must feel if we consider it as settled that when we lie down under the grass there is an absolute end."

I have mentioned the *Mark Rutherford* series because it forms a link in the chain of religious novels, beginning with George McDonald; also because by their great literary excellence they stand alone among their kind. But these books will never be devoured by the "average reader," and for this reason, *Mark Rutherford* cannot be spoken of as one of the popular guides. He is, indeed, *caviare* to the general: the "average reader" finds himself quickly out of his depth here; the young reader, thank God, knows little of the direful experiences recorded in these sombre pages. The rootless intellectual difficulties of youth are

Stones from a Glass House

almost entirely theoretical, and cannot be named in the same breath with the heart-sickening doubts of later life. The man who, through the extremity of his own suffering, has caught a glimpse of the suffering of the whole world, does not doubt for himself alone. He sees his own grief reflected in a million other lives, and the chances are that he doubts in consequence of that insight—doubts of the reported loving God, the merciful Father, the sharer of man's griefs—doubts of His power who does not stem this frightful torrent of human misery—doubts, finally, if any Eye watches over man's pitiful journey.

In the case of the individual, reaction often follows after agnosticism. And following this rule, "Mark Rutherford's" books were followed by those of a reactionist—Mrs. Humphry Ward. She is not content with "the attitude enjoined by the severest exercise of reason"—she

On Religious Novels

is quite convinced that we know enough to guide ourselves, whatever our theoretical difficulties may be. That terribly talked-about book, *Robert Elsmere*, is the outcome of this belief. As all the world knows, *Robert Elsmere* deals with the question of the divinity of Christ. Robert reaches the crisis of his soul's experience when he confesses· "Every human soul in which the voice of God makes itself felt enjoys equally with Jesus of Nazareth the divine Sonship—and miracles do not happen."

Theologians and thinkers had been arguing over this question of the miracle of miracles for a very long time; but at the publication of *Robert Elsmere* all the world began to argue about it. I do not believe that one half the people who professed to find here an expression of their own difficulties had hitherto given the matter an hour's honest thought. The story was arrestingly told, and a new creed

Stones from a Glass House

has attractions, and off went the proverbial sheep after each other to form a Robert Elsmere brotherhood on the spot—so much for such readers.

But among young readers, who are generally untrained thinkers, the influence of *Robert Elsmere* was much deeper. They found here, not only an expression of their doubts, but a satisfactory and well-reasoned solution of how—the miraculous element being excluded from the Gospels—they might yet remain the rule for holy living. Mrs. Ward writes strictly within rules: thus far her doubter goes, and no farther; the difficulty she tries to meet is this of the miraculous element in the Gospel, and this alone—thus indicating one other phase of doubt, a step more advanced than that of George McDonald.

As I said before, very few people care about abstract truth, but they all care about their individual happiness. In

On Religious Novels

Robert Elsmere a great many people found a recipe for happiness, and this was one of the secrets of the book's popularity. It was no new gospel in one way, indeed—just the well-known, little-regarded truism that we must live for others; but it was presented in a new light—life for others was to be our religion, instead of being the outcome of our religion. No doubt this view of things brought comfort to many a heart: there is no comfort at all to be compared with that which comes from practical work after one has been worrying over theoretical difficulties for a long time. If you cannot accept the miraculous element in the Gospel story *Robert Elsmere* taught, accept its practical teaching, and you will see greater works done in yourself—the miracle of a readjusted life brought into line for the purposes of God for all mankind. There is something about the solemn, thoroughgoing manner of *Robert Elsmere* which

Stones from a Glass House

convinces the reader that the author is entirely sincere in her conviction that here lies the road to righteousness.

Whatever the book may or may not be, it is a very thorough bit of work on its own lines, and the question it discusses has been systematically thought out. It is therefore worthy of the attention it received. But it is the painful duty of one who chronicles the rise of religious fiction to notice the extraordinary popularity of the works of Edna Lyall: this lady rushes in where angels fear to tread. She grapples with the question of the existence of law before that of primordial cells: of where, in the evolutionary chain, the soul came in: she attempts, in short, to solve the insoluble, to answer the unanswerable, to know the unknowable. And the result? Well, the result is exactly what might be expected. That such manifest ineptitude should have met with so much admiration is a sign of the

On Religious Novels

times to be carefully noted. Solomon himself could not have answered these questions—the British public, in tens of thousands, accepts the dictum of Miss Edna Lyall upon them, and seems quite satisfied of its validity. It is a pity for a nation to be priest-ridden, to accept its beliefs too childishly from the hands of even a learned class of men; but it is a much greater pity for a nation to give itself over into the hands of novelists for religious instruction. That the works of Edna Lyall are well intentioned, and that their influence is meant to be elevating and wholesome, cannot be questioned; it is the inadequacy of means to the end which annoys one in reading these books and a host of others, their followers, which shall be nameless. The mysteries of God, the unspeakable riddles of life and being—how can these be dealt with in the happy-go-lucky three-volume style, so fatally fluent, so pathetically self-confident? "To

Stones from a Glass House

plough with a light harrow," as the old saying goes, in the dark fields of our awful, inexplicable world is surely a grave blunder. And any author who seriously proposes to settle the riddles of the universe by a work of fiction—or, for that matter, by a work not of fiction—has most evidently scratched only the surface of his subject. This class of religious novel all comes under the reactionist heading: written in the determination that a way is to be found out of the doubts which modern inquiry has raised, they purport to reconcile science and religion. Products merely of a phase in the progress of thought, their nature is necessarily ephemeral. But in their weakness lies their strength. Just because these books attempt the impossible they are eagerly read on all hands, and their readers fondly imagine that they have here a real solution of their difficulties — an argued solution they will tell you — not the emotional

On Religious Novels

appeal of George McDonald, nor the practical refuge of Mrs. Humphry Ward, not the melancholy incertitude of "Mark Rutherford," but a distinctly argued case, in scientific terms, which neatly and accurately meets every difficulty and overcomes it. I have said before, this is what most people want.

For those who desire to go into the question of Churches—Protestant *versus* Catholic—there is a veritable literature of fiction. But as only the novel of dogmatic tendency comes within the scope of this article, these cannot be noticed, though there are many excellent novels with this purpose.

There remains, however, a further, an ultimate stage of doubt, which, occurring as it does in the individual, is bound to be reproduced in literature, which is the synthetic reflection of thousands of individual minds. *The Increasing Purpose*, by John Lane Allen, gives a picture of doubt

Stones from a Glass House

which has reached the point of entire scepticism :—

"Do you not believe in God?" asked the Professor. "Ah—that question! which shuts the gates of consciousness upon us when we enter sleep, and sits close outside of our eyelids as we waken; which was framed in us ere we were born, which comes fullest to life in us as life itself ebbs fastest. That question which exacts of the Finite to affirm whether it apprehends the Infinite—that prodding of the evening midge for its opinion of the Polar Star!"

The story of this doubter's doubts is told in such beautiful language that the book deserves to live, quite apart from the conclusions arrived at in the second, the constructive, half of it. For these conclusions can hardly be called satisfactory :—

"Science, science! There is the fresh path for the faith of the race. For the

On Religious Novels

race henceforth must get its idea of God, and build its religion to Him, from its knowledge of the laws of His universe. A million million years from now! Where will our dark theological dogmas be in that radiant time? The Creator of life in all life must be studied, and in the study of science least wrangling, least tyranny, least bigotry, no persecution. Our religion will more and more be what our science is, and some day they will be the same."

The reign of law—and beautifully, eloquently expressed. But the one tremendous defect lurks here: the wayfaring man, if a fool, would err therein. More than that, the miserable man will not be comforted thus. There is in *Mark Rutherford* a very ridiculous example of what I mean. A description is given there of the way in which Rutherford tried to reconcile a miserable man to life. The man was a waiter in a cheap restaurant, and was underfed, underpaid, and

Stones from a Glass House

overworked. He had a drunken wife who made his home wretched. To soothe these tragically sordid miseries Rutherford tells the man of the reign of law, the ultimate triumph of science: "We tried to soothe him in every way," Rutherford adds naïvely, when recounting this attempt at comfort. To "soothe" a hungry man, who has a drunken wife, by descriptions of the ultimate triumph of law and order is manifestly absurd. This incongruity must appear to any one who seriously tries to salve the ills and woes of life by any such considerations. These lofty counsels might (perhaps) afford some comfort to a Socrates under the trial of a Xantippe—the average man is more likely to be provoked than soothed by them.

When you consider that each one of the authors whose books I have considered, is only the leader of his or her own especial band of imitators, some idea may be ob-

On Religious Novels

tained of the ramifications of religious fiction. Not a doubt but has its special pleader: not a new faith but has its prophet. And the newer the faith, the poorer the book that is produced by it. One has some patience with the old classic doubter, with his genuine scruples; but the newcomers who quickly renounce their childhood's faith, and with the utmost agility replace it by means of electricity or vegetarianism, theosophy or Christian science, cannot hold our sympathies. It is illiberal and perhaps unfair to say that the new is never true; but for the purposes of serious fiction it is a safe rule to keep to the old paths. No brand-new ideas can be the right material for building a book of. The sifting, testing processes of time are needed to make ideas into usable bookstuff, just as wood needs seasoning before it can make a seaworthy craft. The shrinkage of ideas has to be allowed for·—what seems to fill the public mind and

Stones from a Glass House

dominate knowledge one year, may have shrunk into insignificance before twelve more months have run. This view of things, if practically adhered to, leaves rather a small field for the religious novelist of the future. "The stories have all been told"—an eminent authority tells us; certainly the doubts have all been expressed. Perhaps a truce may be called now—it is time—but the War of Opinions will still go on.

THE SLUM MOVEMENT IN FICTION

THOSE who watch the literary firmament had begun to think that the stars of slum literature were set never to rise again, when behold! new stars, one, two, and three, make their appearance in the heavens, all of them twinkling brightly, and doubtless the forerunners of many yet to come.

The truth is that it is no easy matter to say where any literary movement has its end, because it is always going on into fresh forms just as the public gets tired of the well-worn ones, and we recognise old friends with new faces at every turn. Books have, in fact, a very distinct evolutionary history in most cases, and sporadic appearances are infrequent in the world of letters.

Stones from a Glass House

Now, while it would show quite wicked pride to pretend to an exhaustive knowledge of Slum Literature—its appearance and its evolution—I have watched its later developments with so much attention that perhaps my observations upon these may have some interest for readers who have neither time nor inclination to cope with the scores of novels which represent the movement. It is no light thing to hear even the half that the novelists have to say upon any subject. I do not pretend to have heard more than a third of their much speaking.

Many authors, many modes of presentation; but, in spite of this, it is easy to arrange our authors into distinct "schools," each writing from their own standpoint. The slum and the slum-dweller, then, may be, and have been, treated in (at least) five different ways :—

1. As a moral lesson.
2. As a social problem.

Slum Movement in Fiction

3. As an object of pity and terror.
4. As a gladiatorial show.
5. As an amusing study.

The first of these divisions belongs now to a bygone age; the second and third merge into each other; the fourth has not very many exponents; the fifth is the latest evolution of the whole movement.

"I saw no reason, when I wrote this book," says the author of *Oliver Twist*, "*why the dregs of life should not serve the purpose of a moral* as well as the froth and cream . . . it seemed to me that to draw a knot of such associates in crime as really did exist, to paint them in all their deformity, in all their wretchedness, in all the squalid misery of their lives; to show them as they really were, for ever skulking uneasily through the dirtiest paths of life, with the great, black, ghastly gallows closing up their prospect; turn them where they might, it appeared to me that to do this would be to attempt something which

Stones from a Glass House

was needed, and which might be of service to society."

With these words Dickens prefaced his great excursion into Slum-land; in that decent age when an author still thought that he owed his readers some apology for introducing them into low society. These days are long gone by indeed; quite another race of authors has come up to write about the "dregs of life," and another race of readers, too, for that matter, one of whose characteristics is that it cannot bear the very mention of a moral.

Be that as it may, Dickens, the first modern exponent of slum-life, wrote of it as a moralist, or professed to do so. The earlier Victorian era was given over to curious illusions about many things, and was not fond of calling a spade a spade. We find it difficult to believe that Dickens really thought primarily about the moral of *Oliver Twist*, whatever he said. He

Slum Movement in Fiction

was far too great an artist to do anything of the kind; but the Victorian convention was strong upon him, he must fib a little about his work for decency's sake. In reality, surely, his artist's eye had caught sight, in one ecstatic moment, of the dramatic possibilities that lurked in the "knot of associates in crime," and he must be at them with his pen straightway. Still, he finds an apology necessary, and makes it · " I cannot see why the dregs of life should not serve as a moral," &c. Ah, what a free hand Dickens had had in these present evil days! No apologising, no disguising of his eagerness for his subject. I wonder sometimes that a skeleton hand, grasping a ghostly pen, has not appeared to write upon the walls—well, perhaps just the best slum-story of them all.

But we are all the slaves of our generation for good or evil; and Dickens had to write of the slums as they were conceived of in his day—decently, with restraint,

Stones from a Glass House

leaving the greater part unsaid, and *pointing a moral*. Have you read *Oliver* lately? or do you remember him distinctly enough to establish comparisons between him and his grandchildren of the "nineties"? Such comparisons are laughable enough. How the whole presentation of low life has been turned round about since the publication of *Oliver Twist!* And to notice particulars first, how the speech differs. Every one knows, of course, that the dialect of Dickens' London was not the dialect of ours. But, making all allowance for this fact, we can scarcely forbear a smile when we read the grammatical periods of Nance:—" Thank Heaven upon your knees, dear lady (cries Nance in one of those admirably composed exclamatory passages), that you had friends to care for you and keep you in your childhood, and that you were never in the midst of cold and hunger and riot and drunkenness, and — and something

Slum Movement in Fiction

worse than all—as I have been from my cradle. I may use the word, for the alley and the gutter were mine, as they will be my deathbed!" Now (I know nothing of Cockney dialect but what the novelists have taught me) the lady would be exclaiming more to this effect :—

"Thank yer bloomin' stars, lydie, as you 'ad pals a-lookin' arter yer wen you was a bloomin' kid, an' wa'nt clemmed with 'unger an' goin' on the booze, an' maybe street-walkin', like I've been since I was a kid," &c., &c., &c.

The difference in this respect is certainly sufficiently laughable; yet it may be a matter of question whether the realistic method really conveys its impression much more vividly than the Victorian method. Dialect may be—has been—carried too far, and trusted to too much. For dialect, be it never so accurately done, will not convey character one whit; and Nance, with all her fine

Stones from a Glass House

speeches, stands the test of time *as a character* better than most of the realistically treated figure-heads of modern books.

But it is not in detail so much as in purpose that the difference lies. As I have said, Dickens from the outset is moralising; and that is what no modern author would dare to do for a moment—because no one would read his books if he did. The awful retribution of sin, the hard way of the transgressor, is not what we wish to hear about just now, whatever the public of earlier days liked. It is much more to our taste to read of the triumph of the transgressor and the total defeat of innocency by inexorable fate. If any "modern" had undertaken to write Oliver Twist's memoirs, the story would have put on quite another complexion; Oliver would never have been allowed to extricate himself from the snares of Fagin, but would have gone deeper and deeper into the meshes, spite

Slum Movement in Fiction

of youth, and endeavour after good, and mother's prayers, and everything else; for nowadays we must be "relentless," come what may. *The Moral*, in fact (using the expression in its Victorian sense), is extinct; we recognise the uselessness of asserting that "good always triumphs" in the end, or of denying that the wicked are often much more prosperous than the righteous; so we have stopped writing stories to that effect, and the pendulum has of course swung too far in the opposite direction. Still, the public taste holds firmly to the old convention, as you may see exemplified at the theatre any and every night. The villain is always hissed; the audience has nothing but applause when the virtuous hero is successful; it is only in our books that we reverse this law of taste.

Now morality and religion should go hand in hand, yet it is a curious fact that where religion is brought into slum-books,

Stones from a Glass House

all literary value leaves them; while, as we have seen in *Oliver Twist*, the highest literary standard has been reached when the moral is insisted upon. Impossible to account for this fact, I can only mention it and call to your remembrance a host of half-forgotten story books, the favourites of our childhood. Poor relations these of the slum novel: *Christy's Old Organ*, *Froggie's Little Brother*, &c., &c., &c. How sorely we all wept over these tales in the impressionable days of youth! We thought that death was the saddest thing in the world then, and the pages of these books were positively starred with deathbed scenes of a very pious nature. Alas, between literature and life we have become so callous now that we read dry-eyed of sorrows far more bitter.

Yet, radically and ridiculously apart as these humble stories were from the realistic slum-books of the present day,

Slum Movement in Fiction

they were links in the evolutionary chain none the less. In them the modern spirit of pity was beginning to make itself felt, as distinct from Dickens' attitude to the "dregs of society." In these tender pages we learned a great deal about the sufferings of the poor—in a refined, unrealistic fashion. We were encouraged to wonder what we could do to assuage these sufferings, and the sad victims of poverty and crime were no longer pointed out as beacons—after the Dickens fashion.

But these trembling efforts at slum literature were suddenly pushed aside by a vigorous hand, and the whole school of social reformers sprang into being with *Alton Locke*. What a long reign they have had to be sure—they are reigning still. Surely every unwholesome trade has had its novel; every grievance of the toilers its special pleader in fiction. All honour to the reformers, and long may

Stones from a Glass House

they blossom and bear fruit. What Kingsley began Besant went on into, and a host of smaller writers, well-intentioned but nameless, followed hard upon their masters. Year after year the public return with apparently unsated appetite to the novel of social reform; and it is a healthy sign that this should be the case. Once more we have the old problem dished up in *5 John Street*, that curiously popular book of the day. There is much that is true in this book, but not much that is new. Doubtless the horrors of yet one more unwholesome trade are shown up here in a very dramatic way; but the cure which the author announces for this and all kindred ills is such an old one that it seems rather unnecessary to write a novel in illustration of it. "Whatsoever ye would that men should do to you, do you even so to them likewise," was said once for all many hundred years ago; but the public greet it as quite a

Slum Movement in Fiction

new doctrine, and *5 John Street* sells at an amazing rate. This interest in books which treat of social reform is certainly more healthy than the rush that was made for the two other classes of slum literature I have mentioned—*i.e.* (1) the school of pity and terror, and (2) the school of brutality.

The demand for the first of these is, I hope, explained by the fact that the writers of this school have written so admirably.

It was in 1890 that Gissing brought out that extraordinary book *The Nether World*. This man would seem to have been in hell. Other men crawl to the edges of the pit and look over at the poor devils that writhe in its flames—he has come up out of it, and now, like the man of the parable, would testify to his brethren lest they too enter that place of torment. As no one else has ever done—I would almost venture to prophesy as no one else will ever do—Gissing writes the tragedy

Stones from a Glass House

of Want. It is not written with brutality, and that is why it is so terrible and undeniable. This bald incisiveness beggars the vulgar exaggeration of other writers, who by overstating their case deprive it of effect. As we read we know that every word is true—this is hunger, and heaven help the hungry — this despair indeed —not the glib despair which novelists deal in by the page, but that mortal disease of the mind which is past all cure. Gissing has no gospel of hope to offer his readers. "Work as you will," he says, "there is no chance of a new and better world until the old be utterly destroyed." The "lower orders" are, to his seeing, one huge tragedy: "*A Great Review of the People. Since man came into being, did the world ever exhibit a sadder spectacle?*" he inquires. There is no more awful fate, by his showing, than life in the East End. He writes of travelling "across miles of a city of the damned, such as thought never

Slum Movement in Fiction

conceived before this age of ours; stopping at stations which it crushes the heart to think should be the destination of any mortal," and in this key of almost insane depression *The Nether World* continues from its first page to its last—a terrible book; but one that is deserving of more fame than it ever got.

This was in 1890. In 1892-93 Kipling published his first (and last?) slum story, *Badalia Herodsfoot*, and the school of pity was fairly ushered in. Because, where Kipling goes it is safe to say that many follow. I do not mean to say that a man as clever as Arthur Morrison copies from any one—it is only another instance of the provoking fact that where one clever mind strikes out an idea for itself another is almost certain to be striking out the same idea at the same moment—it is a sort of mental contàgion which has to be reckoned with in literary matters. However that may be, Kipling published

Stones from a Glass House

Badalia Herodsfoot in 1893, and Arthur Morrison published *Tales of Mean Streets* in 1894, and the same spirit and temper ran through them both—humanity at its lowest social ebb, yet exhibiting brilliant, wandering lights of soul. We are well versed in the types now, after several years' instruction in them—they came as a surprise to us in 1894. Henceforward Arthur Morrison became the most prominent exponent of the School of Pity. His *Child of the Jago* continued the tradition at its best, and exhibited the "relentless" modern method very plainly. For here is the story of a boy of originally good, tender instincts, who, like Oliver Twist, is in training for a thief. Does innocence triumph here? Is there a measure of hope and comfort at the close? Impossible. Dicky Perrot—the "Oliver" of our day—has never a chance from the cradle to the grave, and the grave has to swallow him up at the end, because

Slum Movement in Fiction

it is probably the only way left for the author to take with his character. It is a book of searching interest and great power, of horrible detail, but withal of deepest pity. We all read the books of Arthur Morrison, and shuddered over them; some people were apparently reading them without the shudder, for in 1897 appeared yet another recruit to the ranks of slum literature, who, in slang phrase, seemed to be determined to "go one better" than his predecessors. The brutal school had appeared. "The vituperative vernacular of the nether world," says George Gissing, "has never yet been exhibited by typography, and *bresumably never will be*"—but this prophecy was too sanguine; some years later Mr. Gissing would not have been so sure about what typography might be called upon to produce. There is practically now no limit to what may be done in this way—unless, indeed, we are forced to start a censor of novels as

Stones from a Glass House

well as of plays. *Liza of Lambeth* saw the light in 1897. It is a story of brutal frankness and sickening import, and has, alas, too surely set a fashion for this sort of thing. We are spared nothing: the reek of the streets; the effluvia of unwashed humanity; but worse than all these outside things is the hopeless moral atmosphere in which the characters move. There are no wandering lights here, the moral darkness is unpierced by so much as a ray of brightness. Nor does the author seem to write in any spirit of pity, or with any love for the creatures he has made. With a stolid indifference he chronicles their hopeless sufferings; without apparent disgust he details the loathsome vices which degrade them; the whole thing is so gratuitous. Why all these horrors? Why all this filth? Such recitals cannot even be defended from the point of view of art, setting aside any question of morality—and, books being

Slum Movement in Fiction

primarily supposed to be works of art, this should be the deepest condemnation that can be passed upon any work. Now this brutal—gratuitously brutal—class of book stands accused by its entire lack of light and shade, its continual overstrain. Such work is like a man who shouts at the pitch of his voice and calls the noise he produces music; or like the daubs of colour a child covers his paper with, calling it a picture. All intelligence leaves any so-called art when it is without light and shade, and where intelligence is left out art ceases to exist. It is perhaps only fair to admit that inartistic as such work may be, it has a horrid power of its own. This is the very reason, however, why it should be swept away root and branch. It is exactly the same thing in a lesser degree for us to sit down deliberately to read these books, as it was for the much-blamed crowds of sightseers to flock to the bull-fights at Boulogne. The same

Stones from a Glass House

love of "a new shiver" is the explanation of our interest in these horrors—or, perhaps, the aboriginal thirst for blood and violence which is said to lurk in every one of us.

I have remarked that these pictures of slum-life are inartistic—we might still consider it a painful duty to read them if they were true. For it is, no doubt, a good thing to know how half the world lives. But this is just where these books fail. Life in the slums has its joys quite as surely, if not as evidently, as life in palaces, and it is ridiculous to suppose that it has not.

This was a fact which was working obscurely in the writings of Arthur Morrison. *The Child of the Jago* scarcely admits the joys of slum-life, but it gives a fair idea of its pleasurable, if savage, excitements — the ecstasy of Dicky Perrot's absorption in the prize-fight, the lust of battle, the gratulation of successful thiev-

Slum Movement in Fiction

ing — all these dubious joys are freely admitted.

But it remained for yet newer recruits to the slum-writers to discover what I venture to say is more nearly the ultimate truth about slum-dwellers, and to describe this. *'Mord 'Emly* and *The Hooligan Nights* both give voice to this new discovery, and with admirable art, that is quite without exaggeration, show the wild joys and excitements of slum-life. It is no unthinking optimist, but a shrewd observer of human nature, who describes the desperate gloom of 'Mord 'Emly when she finds herself in the respectable suburban kitchen, far from the gay life of her native slum. None of us can do anything but sympathise with her when she makes her wild "break" for liberty and returns, like a homing pigeon, to the haunts of childhood. What else would she do? Where else would she be? And, after all, 'Mord can hold up her

Stones from a Glass House

head with the best of us, though she does live in the "nether world" and dearly loves a street fight. There comes the truth; every slum-dweller is not entirely depraved, or desperately miserable—and Mr. Pett Ridge, by boldly breaking away from the tragic convention of the slums, has come into a new kingdom. But, as I have already pointed out, no man reigns long alone in any literary kingdom; and Mr. Clarence Rooke has entered into possession along with Mr. Pett Ridge. And, again, following precedent, the former exaggerates in *The Hooligan Nights* the joys of slum-life till we are fain to ask, "Who would now be honest?" For, by his showing, "Young Alf," the Hooligan, has a much better time of it than honester men. There is little to deplore in Alf's lot: not much want; no dulness; plenty of excitement; no hard work. And, withal, Alf is such an engaging young man. We

Slum Movement in Fiction

hope he will burgle our house if it is to be burgled, for we would scarcely mind his doing so, and certainly would meet him quite unconcernedly at dead of night. Indeed, we wish Alf all joy in his profession.

To my way of thinking, these later contributions to slum literature are probably more near the truth in their picture of slum-life than any of their predecessors, yet it may be seriously questioned whether all attempts in this sort are not vain? The difference between the educated and the uneducated is as great, Dr. Johnson said, as that between the living and the dead—a statement which may be an exaggeration, but which, coming from such an authority as it does, should be carefully considered by those who try to write the histories of the uneducated classes. The gulf is indeed one which it is curiously difficult to bridge over. We may believe as firmly as we like that we are brothers

Stones from a Glass House

or sisters "under our skin," yet remain in heathen ignorance all the while of the real truth about each other. What we mutually *see* must always be only the surface of things, and anything beyond that no more than clever conjecture. Let us say, then, that the probabilities seem to be with the latest contributors! They avoid successfully the weak points where their predecessors have broken down, are not too moral, or too boring about reform; or too hopelessly tragical, or too desperately brutal; they take, in fact, the middle road of proverb with good results.

THE SCOT OF FICTION

UNTRAVELLED people, who cannot move about the world much, get a dangerous number of ideas of other lands and nations out of novels. Considered as guide-books, it is true that a good deal of reliable information may be got out of modern novels, because the craze for so-called local colour, of which we hear so much just now, fosters habits of accurate observation and description in the writers of the day. But in the matter of national character-drawing fiction still leaves a great deal to be desired. There can be no doubt that novelists are tempted to fall into ruts of character-drawing, so that with long practice types of Scotch, Irish, Cornish, or American character can be produced to order, as a pudding is com-

Stones from a Glass House

pounded from a recipe. It cannot be denied that there are such things as racial characteristics, and this fact is a terrible snare to some authors. It is so much easier to use the accepted types, for instance, of Scotch or Irish character, than to invent or to be at the trouble of observing new and hitherto undescribed characters. Moreover, the general public will, in nine cases out of ten, admire the stereotyped bit of character-drawing more than the newly-observed one—and why, the poor author asks, should the public not get what they like?

I have noticed that some nations seem to lend themselves more easily to this sort of conventional treatment than others, just as certain faces lend themselves to caricature; and to follow out the simile, it is of course those nations with pronounced features of character that suffer most in this way. Take as an instance of this the " New England type": there must

The Scot of Fiction

be in that wide dominion many thousands of different types of character, but the "type" of fiction is always the same:—an austere old maid, heroic, epigrammatic, frugal, and sorrowful, who seems to sit eternally sewing rag carpets except when she is going to "meetin'"; we all know her and her like now, and look for her appearance in every New England story as we look for flowers in May. We get the idea that New England is peopled solely with maiden ladies; till we wonder how the race is continued at all! This insistence upon racial characteristics points to very shallow observation in the authors who practise it; any one can notice these surface similarities, but to find fresh soil it is necessary to pierce down deep below the surface and discover the eternally and curiously individual mind of each man or woman.

For this very reason, as I have noticed above, stereotyped pictures of character

Stones from a Glass House

are far more popular than fresher ones: the public like to find in books what they have observed themselves, and for one man who sees below surface similarities, there are twenty who see nothing else.

Among conventional types, none has been more thoroughly established in the popular mind than the so-called "Scotch character"—and this not only, or indeed so much, in Scotland as all over the world. To many Englishmen there is but one Scotsman—the fictitious Scot—the Scot of fiction. He is a peculiarly odious person: grim, unmannerly, over-religious, hypocritical, grasping, coarse, and miserly—a being to be shunned and feared alike. This phenomenal and fictitious Scot has also a conventional life-story which, with a few variations, has been described over and over again in fiction. He generally begins life as an intelligent herd-boy; then he has to go to school, so that that awful stock figure the Dominie may "walk on."

The Scot of Fiction

(A Scotch story without a dominie is extremely rare — I can remember eight dominies of curious similarity as I write.)

From the village school the herd-hero migrates to London with strange insistency. Before doing so, however, he must have fallen in love with the laird's daughter: this is a necessary part of the construction of the tale in every case. Arrived in London, the extraordinary career of this prodigy begins: the woolsack looms ahead; he maintains in the meantime all the frugal habits learned at home, always grudging even a sixpence for his own use, but habitually posting his weekly savings to his saintly mother. (Those Scottish mothers!) Struggles and parsimony are of course always in fiction crowned by success, whatever may be the case in fact; so we very speedily find our hero returning rich and distinguished to his native land and village to marry the laird's daughter, rescue the dominie from drink and despair, and fold

Stones from a Glass House

the sainted mother to his heart in an ecstasy of filial devotion. Throughout this career the Scot of fiction keeps up the habit of church attendance in Babylon the great, and enters upon long discussions, in season and out, of predestination and election.

This is the generally received idea of the typical Scot: his career and his character, which from the days of Galt downward has been repeated with many variations; the aspiring, miserly, dutiful, religious, argumentative hero has in fact become a convention. It is a great pity that this should be the case. For though there is a degree of plausibility in this kind of characterisation, it is essentially shallow. A certain number of Scotsmen may seem to conform to this type; but the similarity is only on the surface, as a more careful study of human nature would soon show. In the classical Scotch novelists, Scott and Ferrier, you will never find stock figures of

The Scot of Fiction

typical Scotsmen; each portrait is that of an individual; whereas the Scot of modern fiction is apt to be like a composite photograph where the features of half-a-dozen men are jumbled together to form one face. Scott's most brilliant characters, such as Dominie Sampson (how far from the typical dominie!)—poor Peter Peebles, Cuddie Headrigg, or Dandie Dinmont, are such perfect portraits of *individuals*, that they might find their representatives in any nation. Their qualities are common to the whole human species, not only to the natives of North Britain. The same may be said of Miss Ferrier's brilliant caricatures — Lady Maclauchlan, Mrs. Major Wadell, and Miss Pratt have their counterpart in many lands.

The forerunner of the modern school of Scotch writers was Galt—a sinner above the common in the over-emphasis of racial characteristics. There is no doubt that

Stones from a Glass House

Galt's novels have gone far to establish the unpleasant popular idea of the Scottish character. He is very unfair to his countrymen: all his vital characters—those that make his books—are singularly unlovely. Those that are meant to be good are very vulgar; those that are bad are not credited with one redeeming quality. Galt has in fact set himself unflinchingly to the depiction of all the racial faults. Greed, coarseness, meanness, are his constant themes. The unpleasant characteristic of "nearness" he emphasises to an altogether unnecessary extent. His men and women are all misers: one would gather from these books that no Scotsman ever spent a penny ungrudgingly, or even a halfpenny; that he grasps by fair means or foul from his nearest and dearest, and goes down into the grave clutching the money bags still.

This is an entirely untrue and exaggerated picture of Scotch character; yet

The Scot of Fiction

it has influenced the best modern writers. The belief in Scotch meanness has deepened into such a convention that any writer professing to write a "Scotch" story without making his hero mean, would be jeered at as no true portrayer of the national character. Stevenson—of all the school of modern Scotch novelists the least prone to "stock" characterisation—could not resist the convention, and must make David Balfour grudge his sixpences.

Now, I do not deny that our nation is fond of a bargain, but to call it a nation of misers is unjust. Moreover, the heroic side of the national frugality might just as well be shown, and with far more truth and justice. For one miser in Scotland there are fifty men whose frugality is infinitely noble; and it is well to remember the historic pathos that underlies the racial frugality. Poverty was our poor Scotland's burden for many centuries, and if her men and women are careful now, it is

Stones from a Glass House

from an instinct inherited through generations of half-starved ancestors whose heroic struggles never kept the wolf at any great distance from the door.

The next convention which is firmly established in the popular imagination, and fostered by the novelists, is the predestination and election jest. In "Scotch" novels few Scotsmen speak many words without bringing in some doctrinal allusion, as: "Gin ye had cuttit yersel' wi' yer ain razor, wad *effectual callin'*, think ye, be the first word in yer mouth?" (*Lilac Sunbonnet*, p. 68); or: "Ye ken verra weel that we're a' here on probation, *and that few are chosen—just a handfu' here an' there*," said Milton. "*Verra comfortin' for the handfu'*, said Jamie" (*The Days of Auld Lang Syne*, p. 322). Now this is a perfectly false and ridiculous misrepresentation. You may travel from one end of Scotland to another and never hear predestination

The Scot of Fiction

or election mentioned, yet conventions die so hard, that nothing will convince your average Englishman of this, and he will support his belief by pointing to certain novels, the work of Scotsmen, who agree in depicting their fellow-countrymen after this fashion. This convention probably had its origin in the fact that Scotch people undoubtedly find theological questions more interesting than do their English neighbours. This being the case, it was easier, for purposes of fiction, to epitomise this interest into these two great questions of predestination and election, just as a designer will for purposes of decoration exaggerate some one characteristic of a flower at the expense of all its other attributes. An effective design is produced in this way, but it is not the true picture of the flower by any manner of means; and in the same way the typical Scot, who is always talking about election, makes an

Stones from a Glass House

effective figure in fiction, yet is very far removed from the real Scot of flesh and blood, who is too intelligent to be puzzling himself at this time of day over bygone questions of this kind He is more likely to be "exercised" over the Higher Criticism or theories of Inspiration, for he is nothing if not progressive; if he has doubts at all, be sure they will be doubts of the modern kind.

How little this very marked characteristic of Scottish character has been insisted upon, we have only to glance over some "Kailyard" novels to see: the old doubts, the old difficulties, the old beliefs, are everywhere spoken of—of the newer thought, the constant spirit of inquiry, unresting, out-going, progressive, we never hear. Yet the latter is the true picture of modern Scotland, the former is the most outworn convention—a picture perhaps of a bygone generation, but certainly not of the men of these days.

The Scot of Fiction

Among modern writers Galt has a true follower in the late George Douglas, author of that remarkable book, *The House with the Green Shutters*. Mr. Douglas follows Galt in his unsparing exposure of the national faults of the Scottish people. All the most hideous characteristics of the race are hauled out into the light and exhibited with brutal callousness. "Hateful and hating one another" might have been the motto of this horridly clever book. It seems to have been specially written to exhibit the sin of Spitefulness almost merging into Hate :—

"For many reasons intimate to the Scotch character," says Mr. Douglas, "envious scandal is rampant in petty towns such as Barbie. To go back to the beginning, the Scot, as pundits will tell you, is an individualist His religion alone is enough to make him so. For it is a scheme of personal salvation significantly described by the Rev. Mr.

Stones from a Glass House

Struthers of Barbie. 'At the Day of Judgment, my friends,' said Mr. Struthers, 'at the Day of Judgment every herring must hang by his own tail.' Self-dependence was never more lucidly expressed. History, climate, social conditions and the national beverage have all combined to make the Scot an individualist, fighting for his own hand. The better for him if it be so; from that he gets the grit that tells. From their individualism, however, comes inevitably a keen spirit of competition (the more so because Scotch democracy gives fine chances to compete), and from their keen spirit of competition comes, inevitably again, an envious belittlement of rivals. If a man's success offends your individuality, *to say everything you can against him is a recognised weapon of the fight.* It takes him down a bit, and (inversely) elevates his rival."

What an indictment is this! And the author from beginning to end of his book has the same accusation to make. The

The Scot of Fiction

village gossips of Barbie collect to watch the drunkenness of one of their number: "*He was drunk; but not as drunk as they had hoped.*" Or again :—

"A pretended sympathy, from behind the veil of which you probe a man's anguish at your ease, is *a favourite weapon of human beasts anxious to wound.* The Deacon longed to try it on Gourlay. Never a man went forth, bowed down with recent shame, wounded and wincing from the public gaze, but that old rogue hirpled up to him and lisped with false smoothness, 'Thirce me, neebur, I'm thorry for ye! Thith ith a *terrible* affair! It'th on everybody'th tongue. But ye have my thympathy, neebur, ye have tha-at'—and, all the while, the shifty eyes above the lying mouth would peer and probe, to see if the soul within the other was writhing at his words."

The book has all the qualities of a savage caricature—the unmistakable like-

Stones from a Glass House

ness, coupled with hideous distortion. For it cannot be denied that some of the "Barbie" characteristics may be found in many Scotsmen; but that they are as universal as Mr. Douglas would make us believe, is a libel not on Scotland only but on human nature.

It is almost ridiculous to turn, by way of contrast, to Mr. Barrie's *Window in Thrums*. Thrums is indeed the antithesis of Barbie to an extent that falsifies the one picture or the other as we choose to accept them; they cannot both be true. In Mr. Barrie's village, the natives are so linked together in love and fellowship that, like Christian in the *Pilgrim's Progress*, they seem "as it were in heaven before they came at it." If one author gives too great prominence to the national failings, the other may justly be accused of ignoring too entirely the dark side of Scottish village life. Dear as Mr. Barrie's books must always be to Scotch

The Scot of Fiction

readers, this fact is undeniable. There is little or no mention made of the drunkenness which is the national disgrace, of the unchastity which is making the agricultural districts of Scotland a byword, of the dirt which is all too noticeable on every side. These outstanding faults of our nation are little dwelt upon by the newer storytellers, of whom Mr. Barrie is chief. The cottages are all trim and clean, the women wear spotless mutches, the husbands sit in the ingle-neuk reading the Bible, the ploughmen chastely court the "out-field" workers with honourable marriage full in view

The modern convention of "tenderness," too, may be justly called in question. Your true Scotsman will do his duty to the death for the most unworthy parents; but he will not exhibit much tenderness in the process. I scarcely like to quote Mr. Barrie in a seeming spirit of derision, because his books are de-

Stones from a Glass House

lightful; but to show the difference in his views of the filial relationships from that held by Scott, note the following extracts.

Says Mr. Barrie :—

"Jamie's eyes were fixed on the elbow of the brae, where he would come in sight of his mother's window. Many, many a time I know the lad had prayed God for still another sight of the window with his mother at it. So we came to the corner . . . and before Jamie was the house of his childhood, and his mother's window, and the fond anxious face of his mother herself. My eyes are dull, and I did not see her, but suddenly Jamie cried out, 'My mother!' and Leeby and I were left behind. When I reached the kitchen Jess was crying, *and her son's arms were round her neck.*"

In *Old Mortality* we find the mother and son of the elder novelist's fancy—or perhaps it would be better to say, of his observation :—

The Scot of Fiction

"As soon as Cuddie thought her ladyship fairly out of hearing, he bounced up in his nest. 'The foul fiend fa' ye, that I sud say sae,' he cried out to his mother, 'for *a lang-tongued clavering wife*, as my faither, honest man, aye ca'ed ye! Couldna ye let the leddy alane wi' yer whiggery? And I was e'en as great a gomeril to let ye persuade me to lie here amang the blankets '

"'Oh, my bairn . . .' began Mause.

"'Weel, mither,' said Cuddie, interrupting her, *'what need ye mak' sae muckle din aboot it.'*"

Here the true observer of Scottish manners and characteristics speaks. The average Scot is nothing if not uncivil—he is uncivil even when he means to be respectful; it is part of the independence of his character. The modern writers are far too merciful in their depictions of "manners." I fear the unsuspecting traveller who crosses the Border for the

Stones from a Glass House

first time expecting to meet with the civilities described in modern fiction, will receive a shock!

The time is ripe for a new Scotch novelist who will write of Scotsmen as they are, and not as they are supposed to be: the typical Scot we have had enough of and to spare. But of course the question rises, "What bit of Scotland may the new novelist write about?" for our country is already pretty well laid out after the fashion of gold land, in "claims," to each of which the owner alone has rights. All land north of Inverness, for instance, has been appropriated by William Black; Argyle and the Isles are the exclusive property of Mr. Neil Munro and Miss Fiona Macleod; Ayrshire must be at once renounced to the classic Galt and Mr. George Douglas; Galloway seems a wide country, but the stalwart Mr. Crockett would certainly defend his "claim" by right of might! The Lothians

The Scot of Fiction

are holy ground, Scott and Stevenson surely reign alone there. In Forfarshire Mr. Barrie is king, and Perthshire owns no other lord than "Ian Maclaren." Aberdeenshire was long ago exploited by Mr. William Alexander.

The novelist of the future, then, will need to confine his efforts within a narrow radius. I think (but may be mistaken) that some small tract of country between Banff and Elgin does not belong to any one in especial.

But the Scottish people remain. Thousands of men and women each as different from the other as black is from white, with all the vigour, the intellectuality, the nerve of their race; with its vices too; a strenuous people, capable of anything. This should be an inspiring thought to the story-teller. He need not limit his Scotsman's story to hard probabilities, for there is that in the composition of the race which makes every man and

Stones from a Glass House

woman of them capable of extraordinary possibilities and even impossibilities—a sort of outward-going force, not to be reckoned with or held in check, not to be contained either, be it said, in all the pages of all the novelists put together.

O TEMPORA! O MORES!

THE newly published *Life of Charlotte Yonge* is not an exciting book, yet it is, from one point of view, extremely interesting and suggestive. It is the life of one of the most popular authoresses of the nineteenth century—an authoress whose name has become the proverbial "household word" in most British homes, and whose influence over millions of readers has been far-reaching and enduring.

Yet, on the face of them, these novels by Charlotte Yonge are merely simple tales for young people, of more or less domestic interest and of unvarying moral purpose. Such stories published just now would receive scant notice even from young readers, and none at all from those

Stones from a Glass House

older and more critical in taste. What, then, has been the secret of Miss Yonge's popularity, and what accounts for the influence she had, and still to some extent has, over her readers?

Miss Yonge had the felicity, granted to only a few writers in each generation, to *create a type*. There is a tendency in human nature to run always to one extreme or another; you will find either a very bad or a very good type of hero the favourite of each generation—there is no place found in public favour for the real man of real life who is neither one thing nor the other. Types, in fact, of necessity, and before they become such, must be extreme instances of the characteristics which they embody Whether Charlotte Yonge had consciously grasped this fact we shall never know; sufficient to see that she acted upon it, and in Sir Guy Morville, the hero of the *Heir of Redclyffe*, created a type of the

O Tempora! O Mores!

good hero which, in popularity, outran all competitors. Just as Charlotte Brontë, years before, had fascinated the world by a wicked hero, and created the "Rochester type," so Charlotte Yonge made "Morvillism" the fashion of the hour. Half the youth of England were modelling themselves on Sir Guy a few years after the publication of the *Heir of Redclyffe*. "The enthusiasm about Charlotte Yonge among the undergraduates of Oxford in 1865 was surprising," we are told, and we hear of regiments where every officer had his copy of the famous novel. The pre-Raphaelite brethren—Rossetti, William Morris, and Burne-Jones—"took Sir Guy as their model" (a model which they followed afar off by all accounts); in fact, the popularity of the book in the most unlikely quarters was extraordinary.

Now, how is it possible to account for this sudden fever of interest in the *Heir of Redclyffe?* Had the book

Stones from a Glass House

really sufficient merit to account for its popularity? There are several answers to these questions; the book which attains wide popularity has not of necessity great merit; but it has, inevitably, *something* in it which appeals to human nature—something universal. To detect this vital spark in a book is to discover the secret of its popularity—not always a very easy matter. The great mass of " popular " authors appeal to the lower side of our universal nature; they know that, roughly speaking, every one is interested in murders, hairbreadth escapes, adventures of every kind, so they select these as their subjects. Another and quite as numerous class acknowledge the universal note that is to be found in divorces, adulteries, rivalries, every manifestation of passion; these themes always secure their audience. But it remains for more subtle minds to discover subjects which are at once universal in their interest and yet unhackneyed.

O Tempora! O Mores!

Far be it from me to name Charlotte Yonge "subtle"; yet in justice to the *Heir of Redclyffe* it must be acknowledged that she has made this very discovery—has found a hero who appeals to a huge audience as being a hero, and yet does not make his appeal through any of the lower and more obvious channels. To have done this is something of an achievement, and proves Miss Yonge to have had a higher order of literary faculty and perception than she is generally credited with nowadays. Yet the secret was an exceedingly simple one; merely the old truth of the eternal attractiveness of virtue. This was not a new discovery; to take the greatest instance of all: who has ever tried to deny the extraordinary attractiveness of the character of Christ, or the power which the story has had, and always will have, even over those who do not regard it as a divine revelation. Simple as this great principle is, Miss

Stones from a Glass House

Yonge showed true literary intuition in applying it to popular uses; she realised that the great mass of mankind worship that perfection which they feel it impossible to attain to in their own lives, and she drew a character accordingly—she popularised virtue. It is impossible to repress a smile when we consider the many perfections and the few studied imperfections of Sir Guy Morville, the hero of the *Heir of Redclyffe*; and the question puzzles us continually, " How does such an impossible character still claim our interest and credence?" For Sir Guy is, in truth, an ideal rather than a real creation. His virtues are almost touchingly ridiculous. When he goes to Oxford he excels himself :—

" It was first proposed that Deloraine (his horse) should go with him, but Guy bethought himself that Oxford would be a place of temptation for William (his groom), and resolved to leave them both at Holywell." (!)

O Tempora! O Mores!

At Oxford his own recreations must have been as innocent as those he desired for William, for they were limited to music and walking:—

"The last, he said, might engross him in the same way, but he thought there were higher ends for music, which made it come under Mrs. Edmondstone's rule of a thing to be used guardedly, not disused."

Such temperance in pleasure at eighteen is almost painful. But the same conscience pursues him through life. To counterbalance these virtues Miss Yonge had to introduce at least one fault into her hero's character, so we are told that he had a temper of terrific violence, though the only indication we have of it is "a flashing eye" and a disposition to fly to the piano and play the "Harmonious Blacksmith" whenever his feelings became too fiery to be trusted. It is all ridiculous and impossible and unreal; and yet the char-

Stones from a Glass House

acter of Guy Morville remains attractive, lovable, admirable throughout—just because it is an effort to describe perfection, the thing we all long after and worship in spite of ourselves!

If, then—as it undeniably is—this worship of perfection is an instinct of our nature, it is curious that, from time to time in the world's history, the popular type of hero should have been so far removed from perfection. I have noticed the type of Rochester hero and his popularity as an instance of this, while in real life neroes we may take Byron as another example that vice may run virtue very close, and even, for the time being, may win the race.

We seem to have come to one of these stages in the history of thought at present; the "good" hero has gone suddenly and completely out of fashion. When I say this, I do not assert that a vicious hero is in fashion at present; but that mere "good-

O Tempora! O Mores!

ness" is at a discount, and the want of this quality is, at present, no disqualification for herodom — granted always that the character has enough of strength to justify his own existence. This is the first and greatest essential in the making of the modern hero, and it is a sign of the times that this should be the case. For it is not altogether strength as a splendid characteristic that is admired, but strength as a means to an end, strength as the road to success—that most worshipped idol of the twentieth century. This is a fact that may be read between the lines of nine out of ten novels of the day—the hero is the successful man, and the successful man is the one who has managed to wring from Fortune's grudging hand—*by any means*—those things which are popularly named her gifts: wealth, fame, popularity. Following this rule, the millionaire hero at present carries all before him. The type is rapidly becoming stereotyped, and this

Stones from a Glass House

richly gilded idol bids fair to be worshipped for many days to come. He is always self-made, the clever carver-out of his own destinies; generally rough, blatant, unscrupulous, but always and under all circumstances forceful and masterful. Let us select at random a few descriptions of this favourite type; they will be found to be curiously alike in their main characteristics. Each hero, you will observe, is a man of affairs—of large pecuniary affairs. The type was first ably drawn by Mr. Anthony Hope in *The God in the Car*, some ten years ago; since then African empire-makers and millionaires have appeared in countless numbers. This was the original embryo:—

"Ruston's first five years of adult life had been spent on a stool in a coal merchant's office, and the second five somewhere in Africa. He came before the public offering in one closed hand a new

O Tempora! O Mores!

empire, asking with the other opened hand for three million pounds."

The Company Promoter is thus discussed:—

"'*Gentleman!* Well, everybody's a gentleman now, so I suppose Ruston's one.'
"'I call him an unmannerly brute. . . . Such an *ugly mug as he's got, too; but they say it's full of character.*'
"'Character! I should think so—enough to hang him on sight.'"

Keep in mind this description, and observe how little it has varied after ten years of use in the mill of fiction:—

"Karl Altham was *a plain man, though impressive*—a man about forty-five, his grey thick hair crowning a strong, clean-shaven, mobile face. *He did not look like a gentleman, but he had a personality*—he stood out from the ruck of men as something bigger, stronger, more important than his fellows."

Stones from a Glass House

The first employment of Karl Altham had been winkle-selling; but when the story opens he is a multi-millionaire of immense importance in American affairs.—(*Pigs in Clover*, by Frank Danby.)

Or again, we find in *Moth and Rust* another of the same—a Mr. Van Brunt, who has "a property in Africa larger than England"—he is, of course, aged forty, tall, powerfully built, clean shaven:—

"*You would never say Van Brunt was a gentleman*, but you would never say he wasn't He seems apart from all class. *He is himself.*"

Van Brunt began his career in a dry-goods store as a variation from winkle-selling or coal-selling!

The strange similarity of these descriptions shows what a hold this type has taken upon the imagination of our day; it seems impossible for some authors to avoid describing it. Sir Guy with his

O Tempora! O Mores!

conscience, his solicitude for the welfare of William, and his well-controlled temper, has disappeared from the ranks of heroes (for the time being), and this strong, unscrupulous, successful African gentleman has full possession of the field. This seems at first sight rather a sad fact, and one which does not say much for the good taste of our generation. But perhaps this is not altogether the case. The truth seems to be that our generation have not ceased to worship perfection in the least, but they have begun to worship another side of it from that which the admirers of Sir Guy admired: progress, energy, force, strength of purpose—these have become cardinal virtues with the youth of our day —have, in short, become synonymous with virtue. The man who is unprogressive, lethargic, weak of will, purposeless, can never be virtuous in their eyes whatever other moral qualities he may possess; so

Stones from a Glass House

it follows that the forceful, successful man must become their hero.

Miss Yonge was not, however, content to create a type of hero all her own; she also created a heroine, and so impressed this type upon the mind of the Young England of the day, that she must have helped to mould the characters of thousands of girls into the same grooves.

The long and extraordinarily prolix series of novels which came from her pen are the very apotheosis of domesticity—in them the domestic woman reigns supreme. Miss Yonge's attitude to life (as we see it reflected here) is much that of a butterfly hovering over a dunghill :— It cannot alight on anything foul, but flits off to settle on the flowers instead. The realities of life are curiously glossed over in these books, which seem to have been to a great extent a picture of their author's life. Poverty, shame, anxiety, disaster— all the sinister shapes that dog the foot-

O Tempora! O Mores!

steps of mankind through the long journey—these seem to have been the merest names to Charlotte Yonge. We find no record of them in the tranquil pages of her life. Disease and death all must know sooner or later, but of other and far graver sorrows we hear nothing. Her existence was calm, sheltered, uneventful, narrow—led in one peaceful Church of England groove, far from the anxious and struggling world where most men and women live. The books which had their genesis in such an atmosphere could scarcely have been other than they are: the characters in these books are born in a good position in life, they live and die in it; if shame and calamity overtake them, be sure that the passages which describe these circumstances will not ring true. For Miss Yonge had read and heard of the shipwrecks of life, but she had never gone through them—she was only truly at home and happy and at her best when she wrote of good,

Stones from a Glass House

happy people living blameless and sheltered lives.

It is in creating this sort of domestic atmosphere that Miss Yonge is unrivalled. Nor is she likely soon to find a rival, for the conditions of life have altered so considerably of late years that novels of " home life " have virtually disappeared, along with the homes that used to inspire them : Miss Yonge dearly loved for subject that now almost obsolete institution "*a family circle*," *i.e.* father, mother, eight or even eleven children ; such a household was her special province. Where do we find the family circle now ? To begin with, the parents are no more those of Miss Yonge's fond fancy—quite different fathers and mothers adorn the family circles of our day, to judge from fiction ; some extracts may illustrate the difference better than anything else :—

" ' It will be natural, Margaret '—says Mrs. May, the mother in the *Daisy Chain*—' it will be natural by-and-by

O Tempora! O Mores!

that you should love some one else better than me, and if I cared for being first, what should I do then?'

"'Oh, mamma!—but I' said Margaret, *'you are always sure of papa.'*"

A healthful state of matters this, indeed—to be always sure of papa; but our generation is not quite so confident about papa, and the dark thought will sometimes obtrude itself, "Are we even quite sure of mamma nowadays?"

Kipling scholars will scarcely need to be reminded of the opening scene of the *Gadsbys* as a modern instance:—

"BEAVER [*rapping at door*]. Captain Sahib has come.

"MISS D. What! Captain Sahib! and I'm only half dressed! Well, I shan't bother.

"MISS T. [*calmly*]. You needn't. *It isn't for us.* That's Captain Gadsby. *He is going for a ride with mamma. He generally comes five days out of seven.*"

Stones from a Glass House

What has brought about this revolution in mothers? Those of Miss Yonge's day were much more likely in the natural course of things to be rivals of their daughters, for they were mothers at a far earlier age than is generally the case at present, when women more often marry at forty than at seventeen. Yet such was not the case. With marriage and maternity Miss Yonge's heroines abandoned all pretensions to youth :—

"'In my best days'—says Violet, the heroine of *Heartsease*—'I was not up to Emma; and now, between cares and children, I grow more dull every day.'

"'Your best days! Why, how old are you?'

"'*Almost twenty-two*,' said Violet; 'but I have been married nearly six years. *I am come into the heat and glare of middle life.*'"

Early marriages were perhaps the explanation of the bygone domestic mother,

O Tempora! O Mores!

and the late unions of the present day may explain the modern mother and her foibles—had she, like poor Violet, begun "cares and children" at seventeen, she might indeed feel herself in the heat and glare of middle life a little sooner than she seems to do just now. As it is, she marries late and is more able to face or to evade the worries of maternity, and in consequence retains her youthfulness of spirit much longer. Be this as it may, the fact remains for all to read that "the new mother" is not the same as the old. Moreover, as we explore the various members of one of Miss Yonge's famous "family circles," we perceive that the new daughter is also strangely different from her sister of forty years ago. The tender passion as it was understood, or at least described, by Miss Yonge, is far other than it would appear to be at present among the sons and daughters of our day As an instance of the bygone

Stones from a Glass House

style of thing, may I quote from the *Heir of Redclyffe* a passage which describes Amy and Guy, their feelings and their intercourse, during their engagement :—

"It was a time of tranquil, serene happiness. It was like the lovely weather, only to be met with in the spring, and then but rarely, when the sky is cloudless and intensely blue. . . . Such days as these shone on Guy and Amy, looking little to the future, or if they did so at all, with a grave, peaceful awe, reposing in the present and resuming old habits—singing, reading, gardening, walking as of old, and that intercourse with each other that was so much more than ever before. It was more, but it was not quite the same; for Guy was a very chivalrous lover; the polish and courtesy that sat so well on his frank, truthful manners, were even more remarkable in his courtship. His ways with Amy had less of easy familiarity than in the time of their

O Tempora! O Mores!

brother-and-sister-like intimacy, so that a stranger might have imagined her wooed, not won. *It was as if he hardly dared to believe that she could really be his own, and treated her with a sort of reverential love and gentleness, while she looked up to him with ever-increasing honour.* . . . When alone with Amy he was generally very grave, often silent and meditative, or else their talk was deep and serious."

So much for lovers of the old school. Let us take a modern couple as a foil and the reader shall judge if things have altered for the better or no—whether the "tender passion" has more worthy exponents just now. I quote from a novel named *Mrs. Craddock*, which has received considerable attention of late :—

" He sat down, and a certain pleasant odour of the farmyard was wafted over Bertha, a mingled perfume of strong tobacco, of cattle and horses; she did

Stones from a Glass House

not understand why it made her heart beat, but *she inhaled it voluptuously and her eyes glittered.* . When he bade her good-bye and shook hands she blushed again; she was extraordinarily troubled, and, as with his rising the strong masculine odour of the countryside reached her nostrils, her head whirled. . . . Above all he was manly, and the pleasing thought passed through Bertha that his strength must be quite herculean. *She barely concealed her admiration.* . . . 'Shut your eyes,' she whispered, and she kissed the closed lids; she passed her lips slowly over his lips, and the soft contact made her shudder and laugh; she buried her face in his clothes, inhaling there masterful scents of the countryside. . . . *She knew not how to show the immensity of her passion.*"

This is Bertha's first love: but she is a woman of volatile affections, for ere the book ends we have another description of

O Tempora! O Mores!

an even more erotic nature—the object of this passion being a Rugby schoolboy :—

"She flung her arms round his neck and pressed her lips to his; she did not try to hide her passion now; she clasped him to her heart and their very souls (?) flew to their lips and mingled. This kiss was rapture, madness, it was an ecstasy beyond description, their senses were powerless to contain their pleasure. Bertha felt herself about to die; in the bliss, in the agony, her spirit failed and she tottered—he pressed her more closely to him."

We may indeed trace the curious difference between Amy and Bertha a little further; for, by a strange coincidence, we find both these ladies in the closing pages of the two books which record their fortunes, occupied in the same manner, *i.e.*, gazing at the mortal remains of their husbands. But though there is a similarity in the situation, you will notice that

Stones from a Glass House

there is a wide divergence in sentiment between the heroines. Amy, the older-established heroine, shall have the precedence in quotation :—

"Amy indulged herself with one brief visit to the room where all her cares and duties had lately centred. *A look—a thought—a prayer. The beauteous expression there fixed was a help*, as it had ever been in life, and she went back again cheered and sustained. She had no time to herself except the few moments that she allowed herself now and then to spend in gazing at the dear face that was still her comfort and joy. . . . She entered the little room where that which was mortal lay, with its face bright with the impress of immortality.

"'Is he not beautiful?' she said, with a smile like his own.

"'My dear, you ought not to be here,' said Mrs. Edmonstone, trying to lead her away.

"'*If you would let me say my prayers here*,' said Amy."

O Temporal O Mores!

This is how Amy comported herself; let us hear Bertha's views of bereavement:—

"After his death Bertha was appalled by the regret which she felt rising within her. Oh, she could not risk the possibility of grief; her only chance of peace was *to destroy everything that might recall him.* She stood in front of the corpse and looked. The impression of the young man passed away, and she saw him, as in truth he was, stout, red-faced, with the venules of his cheeks standing out distinctly in a purple network. . . . The hands which had once delighted her by their strength, now were repellent in their coarseness. For a long time their touch had disgusted her—*this was the image Bertha wished to impress on her mind.*"

It may be objected that Bertha is not so much a typical modern heroine as a sort of freak—that in every generation women of this kind may be found. But I am sorry to say that Bertha is already a

Stones from a Glass House

type in fiction. It would be easy to adduce half-a-dozen authors—popular all of them — whose heroines differ from Bertha in name only. We have not far to look for the reason of this change in heroines—it is the old story of the swing of the pendulum—the rebound which is a law of nature. If Miss Yonge and her generation avoided the realities of life, our authors of to-day emphasise them in a quite unnecessary manner, and the one picture is fully more untrue than the other. It is not possible to take a charitable view of this development in heroines: the masterful hero may be regarded as only another manifestation of the ideal; but by no stretch of charity can the courtesan heroine be viewed in this favourable light. The "oldest profession in the world" certainly furnishes the novelist with many an effective subject; but it seems a pity for the idea to get abroad that every woman is at heart

O Tempora! O Mores!

a rake, or worse. This, without mincing matters, is just what is being taught us on all sides at present. The return to nature, to "reality," is being overdone: in this attempt to analyse the primitive instincts of woman, many of her most inborn characteristics are entirely ignored—for bad as the world is, it would be even worse if faithfulness, purity, and modesty were not unchangeable instincts with the larger proportion of women.

We need then, indeed, a return to nature—to the whole of human nature instead of one side of it—a return, in fact, to some of those simple, undeniable goodnesses which form such a large part of life, and are as truly real, and more so, than half the primordial instincts we hear so much about just now.

THE ART OF NARRATION

THOSE few persons who study literature—who read, that is to say, not altogether for the story of a story, or for the knowledge contained in books of research or of criticism, but take an interest in the form as well as the matter of a book—those persons are always asking themselves questions: "The form is changing—why?" "Is the new form better or worse than the old one?" "What has caused the change?" "Where will the change lead to?" and so on, and so on.

It is in the art of narration that change of form shows more than in any other branch of literature. And by the art of narration I do not mean only story-telling in its usual sense, but also all descriptive writing. For fiction may perish, as the

The Art of Narration

prophets tell us that it will; but while the world goes round, descriptive writing, in one form or another, must ever remain with us. Some one gifted with this art of narration will always be wanted to describe to other people what they either have not seen or could not see for themselves. Now, surely the art has changed its form very materially in our day, and I wish to inquire into this change; to try to account for it; and to plead for the new methods of the art.

The change is from prolixity to brevity; from colourless detail to vivid outline; from long words to short ones. "Skip descriptions" used to be a sort of unwritten law with readers—but descriptions are now condensed into a few exquisitely chosen words which are wedged into the narrative, and can no more be skipped in reading it than the currants in a cake can be omitted in the eating. The diffuse, ready-made, conventionally-adjectived "descrip-

Stones from a Glass House

tion" of the Victorian era has absolutely disappeared among writers who take any literary rank at all. Far more pains are bestowed on a few words of modern description than went to a whole page of so-called descriptive writing in those days. Then it was the reader who had the hardest work to do, not the writer—for what can be a greater mental effort than trying to realise to oneself any scene which is described indistinctly?

The reader of former days was constantly expected to use his imagination, instead of having the picture painted for him so vividly that it required no effort on his part to visualise it.

You will see what I mean if you contrast a descriptive passage from Scott with one from any good modern writer. To gain any impression of the country which Scott is describing, a reader would need to close his eyes and think long and carefully —

The Art of Narration

"The Cheviots rose before me in frowning majesty; not, indeed, with the sublime variety of rock and cliff which characterises mountains of the primary class, but huge, round-headed, and clothed with a dark robe of russet, gaining by their extent and desolate appearance an influence upon the imagination which possessed a character of its own."

Here the reader who is called upon to image the frowning majesty of the Cheviots finds himself, before he has fairly visualised this, confronted with the staggering question: "What are the characteristics of mountains of the primary class?" True, the author supplies the answer, that "a sublime variety of rock and cliff" is their characteristic; but the reader keeps ransacking his brain none the less for half-remembered bits of information about "rocks of the primary class," while his eye goes on reading down the page of the "huge, round-headed" mountains, and he

Stones from a Glass House

wonders what the character of that "influence" might be, which he is told they "exercised upon the imagination."

Or let us take another example—because it is impious to find fault with Scott—and Galt shall furnish the text this time :—

"The year was waning into autumn, and the sun setting in all that effulgence of glory with which, in a serene evening, he commonly at that season terminates his daily course behind the distant mountains of Dumbartonshire and Argyle. A thin mist, partaking more of the lacy character of a haze than the texture of a vapour, spreading from the river, softened the nearer features of the view; while the distant were glowing in the golden blaze of the western skies, and the outlines of the city on the left appeared gilded with a brighter light," &c., &c., &c.

Here not only the construction of the sentence is slovenly to a degree, but the whole manner of relation is intolerably

The Art of Narration

tedious. It is a typical description of that era when authors either could not describe or would not give themselves the trouble to do so. Just read alongside of Galt's wearisome wordiness a line or two from Kipling :—

" The animal delight of that roaring day of sun and wind will live long in our memory—the rifted purple flank of Lackawee, the long vista of the lough darkening as the shadows fell; the smell of a new country, and the tearing wind that brought down mysterious voices of men from somewhere high above us."

Or, to take another "modern instance," can words go farther than this from Stevenson :—

"On this particular Sunday there was no doubt but that the Spring had come at last. It was warm, with a latent shiver in the air that made the warmth only the more welcome. *The shallows of the stream glittered and tinkled among bunches*

Stones from a Glass House

of primroses. Vagrant scents of the earth arrested Archie by the way with moments of ethereal intoxication. The grey, quakerish dale was still only awakened in places and patches from the sobriety of its winter colouring; and he wondered at its beauty; an essential beauty of the old earth it seemed to him . . . and when he had taken his place on a boulder, *near some fairy falls, and shaded by a whip of a tree that was already radiant with new leaves,* it still more surprised him that he should find nothing to write . . . he lingered yet a while in the kirkyard. A tuft of primroses was blooming hard by the leg of an old black table tombstone, and he stopped to contemplate the random apologue. They stood forth on the cold earth with a trenchancy of contrast; and he was struck with a sense of incompleteness in the day . . . the chill there was in the warmth, *the gross black clods about the opening primroses,* the damp, earthy smell that was everywhere intermingled with the scents."

The Art of Narration

These examples of modern description are typical of the new movement at its best; they exhibit all the virtues of the school and none of its vices; but, to be quite impartial, I must point out what these vices are. The first, and most marked, is the over-use of onomatopoetic words.

Now, there is no doubt that the use of a description is to convey its impression vividly, and to this end there is perhaps no cheaper method than the use of words which express themselves. Starting from this basis, repudiating the much used verb, adjective, and adverb of literature, some writers have quite run away with the method, so to speak, and have succeeded in going off the rails of "literature"—of classicality—in consequence of this bolt into unknown paths. Description must be vivid, they say, no matter how the effect is obtained. The results of this departure are rather startling. I quote at random

Stones from a Glass House

from a very typical book of this class—*The Red Badge of Courage* :—

"His canteen *banged* rhythmically and his haversack *bobbed* softly—he *wriggled* in his jacket—the *purple* darkness was filled with men who *jabbered*—he felt the *swash* of the water—his knees *wobbled*—the ground was *cluttered* with men—a *spatter* of musketry—the fire dwindled to a vindictive *popping*—the man was *blubbering*—another man *grunted*—the guns *squatted* in a row like savage chiefs—they argued with abrupt violence, it was a grim pow-wow."

It is all ridiculously effective, expressive, convincing ; but too uncouth by far to be admitted to the high places of literature. There is a very practical working test for language, *i.e.*, to ask whether any other word could have expressed the intended meaning as well; and this test has **not** always been applied here. Many more shapely words would have expressed the

The Art of Narration

meaning admirably without giving offence to the ear, and yet without conveying any impression of primness—that bugbear of modern writers.

Another vice of the less practised followers of the new school is a total want of all construction in their sentences. Because prolixity and over-elaborated phrasing were the snares of bygone writers, that is no reason why we should cut up our sentences into four or five words:— Nothing is easier. The method is simple. It presents no difficulties. It is distinct. It appeals to many. It is new. Therefore it pleases. For a time. But not permanently. Men of intelligence yawn. The trick is too readily seen through. It is like an infant's reader: "My cat is called Tom. Do you like cats? No, I like dogs. I like both cats and dogs," &c., &c.

But this is enough of fault-finding; and every new movement must go through

Stones from a Glass House

some ridiculous phases of growth; and instead of laughing at these we must acknowledge the benefit that the movement has been in the main. Just look at Kipling's language—the masterly way in which he employs words old and new indifferently, but *always the best word*. Try to substitute any other for one chosen by him, and you will quickly recognise his art:—

"A boat came *nosing* carefully through the fog." "Over that *pock-marked* ground the regiment must pass." "Beautiful ladies who watched the regiment in church were wont to speak of Lew as an angel. They did not hear his *vitriolic* comments on their morals and manners as he walked back to barracks."

What an advance there is here from the days when only well-known words were employed—"a shady grove," "a handsome youth," "a graceful girl," "a lofty mountain," "a rapid stream,"—the noun and the adjective were then as inevitably coupled together

The Art of Narration

as B follows A in the alphabet; no one thought of altering the arrangement. The change is sure also to be a lasting good, because it is the outcome of thought, not of fashion—no man, even if he catch up mannerisms of style quickly, can produce fresh adjectives by imitation; this is a bit of work that must always come straight from the author's own brain.

The second great change which I notice in the better class of descriptive writing is that it is almost entirely done by simile. The power of mere words is, when all is said and done, very limited. You may choose your words never so cleverly, but if you trust to words alone you will not get half the effect that can be gained by one good simile. As an example of well-chosen simile, let us quote Kipling once again:—

"The low-browed battleships slugged their bluff noses into the surge and rose *dripping like half-tide rocks.*" "The weather was glorious—a blazing sun, and

Stones from a Glass House

a light swell to which the cruisers rolled lazily, *as hounds roll on the grass at a check."*

This is an example of simile made use of in short, unelaborated description. But it is to Thomas Hardy, who must surely stand out as the very prince of all our modern descriptive writers, that we must look for examples of the constant and elaborate use of simile as a method of heightening effects. He never even attempts to describe without it; having apparently gauged the value of mere words to convey impressions. He seems to consider that our imaginations always need the crutch of simile, and that we can only be made to realise something that we have not seen by the help of something that we have seen. Let me give you two examples of his word-pictures, which are much more exhaustive and quite as unconventional as anything in Kipling, yet, by reason of the travail shown in them, greater incomparably. The elaboration

The Art of Narration

without tediousness in the following description is a marvel of workmanship. And notice the constant use which is made of simile :—

"They could then see the faint summer fogs in layers, *woolly* level, and *apparently no thicker than counterpanes*, spread about the meadows in detached remnants of small extent. On the grey moisture of the grass were marks where the cows had lain through the night—*dark green islands* of dry herbage the size of their carcases in the general sea of dew . . . or perhaps the summer fog was more general, and the meadows lay *like a white sea*, out of which the scattered trees rose *like dangerous rocks*. Birds would soar through it into the upper radiance and hang on the wing, sunning themselves, or alight on the wet rails subdividing the meads, which now shone *like glass rods*. Minute diamonds of moisture from the mist hung, too, upon Tess's eyelashes, and drops upon her hair, *like seed pearls*."

Stones from a Glass House

Or again:—

"There had not been such a winter for years. It came on in stealthy and measured glides, *like the moves of a chess-player.* One morning the few lonely trees and the thorns of the hedgerow appeared *as if they had put off a vegetable for an animal integument.* Every twig was covered with a white nap, *as of fur grown from the rind during the night,* giving it four times its usual dimensions; the whole bush or the tree *forming a staring sketch in white lines on the mournful grey of the sky and horizon.* Cobwebs revealed their presence on sheds and walls where none had ever been observed till brought out into visibility by the crystallising atmosphere—hanging *like loops of white worsted* from salient points of the outhouses, posts, and gates."

Description can go no farther. And here are all the best qualities of the new school of writers grouped together—vividness, minuteness without prolixity (for who would wish one detail omitted?), free use

The Art of Narration

of words wherever derived, and with it all exquisite selection.

Now, I have given enough of examples to prove that the change in descriptive writing is really accomplished; but it is more difficult to say exactly what has caused the change.

I am inclined to think that though it is in part a literary movement, it owes a great deal to another cause. There is a well known saying that "the demand creates the supply," which may give us some clue to all this change. This is an impatient, nervous generation — over-busy, over-stimulated; and unless a writer can write a description which interests the reader *in spite of himself*, he had better not write at all. The author who appeals to an overworked, nervous reader is one who conveys his meaning almost instantaneously to the reader's mind without effort on his part. This is what really good descriptive writers can do: it is what the best writers

Stones from a Glass House

of the new school do. Perhaps the inherent love of novelty that there is in all of us is also an element in the new movement. We would rather have any change than none, and style has to come under this law as surely as every other art; but, as I have pointed out, this word-revolution is one which has been brought about thinkingly, so it is likely to prove a permanent one, not a mere rebellion against the powers that be.

Some critics are a little apt to assert that nothing new can be classic; which is just as foolish as it is to say that everything old is classic. It remains with the younger men of the new school to show that their work may take as high rank, for all its newness, as the great work of long ago. And this not only in spite of its revolutionary tendencies, but by reason of them.

GEORGE BORROW

THERE has been of late a great rising again from the shelves of George Borrow. Every magazine has its article upon him, and the tardy publisher at last begins to advertise the much-needed "new and complete" edition of George Borrow's works. All this is consequent upon the publication of Dr. Knapp's *Life of Borrow*—the first authentic life of the man which has appeared since his death in 1881.

Now it is more than fifty years since the Borrow books were published—time enough, surely, for a reputation to be made; time enough even for it to be made and forgotten and made over again; and this is a good deal what has happened to Borrow's reputation in these fifty years. *The Bible in Spain*, and *Lavengro*, and

Stones from a Glass House

Romany Rye created an immense sensation in their day, yet it is a surprising fact that even among people who profess an interest in books and are well read in modern literature there is a large class who only know Borrow by name. "Oh yes, he wrote about gipsies," is the usual uninterested answer such people give when asked if they know anything about him. Indeed, a vague impression exists in some quarters that Borrow was a sort of lay evangelist, who went about scattering Bibles among the gipsies, and then wrote an account of their conversions. *The Bible in Spain* was perhaps the most ill-advised title that a well-written book ever laboured under, giving as it does the idea that the book is a prolonged tract.

But the new *Life*, and the interest that it has created, will surely send readers to the books themselves to get all their false impressions put to rights; *after* reading

George Borrow

them is the time to read the *Life*, and not till then. This provokingly exhaustive *Life* tells us exactly what we do not wish to know; and it has reticences which the true admirer of Borrow feels to be almost an insult. We open it, full of interest, confident that we shall find here the solution of a great many puzzles: and we do not find it. Dr. Knapp tells his readers at once as much and as little as it is possible to tell them. That is to say, he gives aggravatingly precise dates and lists of dry-as-dust details, while he tells us nothing at all about the real George Borrow. Does any one care to have a list of all the boys who were at school with Borrow at Norwich; or to have a dated list of everything he ever penned, known or unknown; or to be presented with a facsimile of the first advertisement of *Romany Rye?* Such trivialities are purely teasing in a biography, which should be plainly what it is—nothing

Stones from a Glass House

more or less than a story. The biographer who makes his hero a hero is the successful writer of lives; and no one who cannot do this should essay the task. Nor should the real biographer resent as curiosity the reader's wish to know the truth about the man he reads of; unless the truth is told in a life it had better not be written, and to suppress facts just because they do not reflect credit upon the subject of them is necessarily to falsify the whole character-sketch. Dr. Knapp perhaps does not actually suppress, but he draws a curtain down with great determination every here and there, always just as the scene is getting interesting. Could there be a surer way than this of bungling a biography?—to tell every unnecessary detail and omit every vital fact.

However, one must "take what one gets and be thankful," as the old proverb says, in the way of biography, that least understood of all the perplexing paths of

George Borrow

literature. For the generally received idea is that any one can write a life if given the facts, and until that grievous mistake is corrected, we must just read dull lives of clever men with patience, waiting for the clever men to rise who will be able to write even the lives of dull ones amusingly.

Dr. Knapp's object then, in spite of his worship of George Borrow, seems to have been to make him entirely prosaic in the eyes of his readers. There is not a hint even of interest or of romance in these two great volumes. And this is the life of George Borrow, the prince of adventurers, whose books read like a long fairy tale written for grown-up people! All the burning questions which we have on our lips after reading the Borrow books remain unanswered when we have finished the *Life:* "What did he do in 'the veiled period'—those mysterious seven years that are omitted from the *Life?*"

Stones from a Glass House

"Who was Isopel Berners?" "Did he ever meet her again?" "Was Borrow mad?" "Was he a humbug, or did he really take an interest in the Bible Society?" "Was he happily married to his elderly wife, or did he marry for money?" All these facts may be too sacred for publication, but if they are, then the man's whole life was unsuited for a profane public to investigate into, and the *Life* should never have been published.

I am confident, however, that Borrow's admirers who *first read all his books* and then read his *Life* will form their own (perhaps mistaken) theories upon his life. They will know well enough whether he ever met Isopel Berners again; and whether he was happily married; and whether he was mad; and what he did in the "veiled period." And it is certain that these theories, one and all, will be quite different from the suggestions which

George Borrow

are thrown out in the *Life* by discreet Dr. Knapp.

But I have been writing all this time as if all my readers had read Borrow's life and his books; while the chances are that many of them have read neither, and therefore are quite in the dark about them both. For the enlightenment of people in this enviable state of darkness —enviable because they have such pleasures in store—I must give some details of Borrow's life, and explain why it deserved to be written and why his books should be read and remembered.

George Borrow was born at East Dereham in 1803. He was the son of a recruiting officer, and when quite a child was taken by his parents all over England, Scotland, and Ireland, never settling down for any length of time in one place; at last he was sent to complete his very desultory education at a school in Norwich, and finally was articled to a solicitor of that

Stones from a Glass House

town in 1819. But the boy's real talent was for languages, not for law; he learnt "any language in six weeks," as his boast was; so early in life he began to dabble in translation, turning off English versions of Danish and Welsh poems, which did not prove very saleable. Then, after the traditional way of clever youth, Borrow went up to London, and lived there "from hand to mouth," doing hack work for a publisher, till he started suddenly off on those travels through England which are described in *Lavengro*, the most delightful of all his books. Having starved and struggled long enough in towns, he resolved that he would starve in the wide green country now, and not struggle after a livelihood or fame any longer. So through the dear English lanes he travelled, picking up an existence somehow, and falling in (by his own account) with extraordinary adventures. *Lavengro* tells us all these stories, and as

George Borrow

we read it we are lifted into an atmosphere of sudden romance. The lanes are peopled not with the work-a-day men and women of our world, but by a race of beings unlike any we have ever met. We find them speculating on curious themes in strange language, and it would appear that every wayfarer Borrow met had some odd contribution to make either to his knowledge or to his philosophy. Borrow is always asking questions; it is his "method" of character-sketching; and by the time he has cross-examined his witness, there he stands before the reader more distinctly drawn by his own replies than if Borrow had spent a page of description upon him:—

"'What is your opinion of death, Mr. Petolengro?' said I, as I sat down beside the gipsy.

"'My opinion of death, brother, is much the same as that in the old song of Pharaoh, which I have heard my

Stones from a Glass House

grandam sing: "When a man dies he is cast into the earth, and his wife and child sorrow over him . . . and if he is quite alone in the world, why, then he is cast into the earth and there is an end of the matter."'

"'And do you think that is the end of a man?'

"'There's an end of him, brother, more's the pity.'

"'Why do you say so?'

"'Life is sweet, brother.'

"'Do you think so?'

"'Think so! There's night and day, brother, both sweet things; sun, moon, and stars, brother, all sweet things; there's likewise a wind on the heath Life is very sweet, brother; who would wish to die?'

"'I would wish to die.'

"'You talk like a Gorgio, which is the same as talking like a fool—wish to die, indeed! A Romany chal would wish to live for ever!'

"'In sickness, Jasper?'

George Borrow

"'There's the sun and stars, brother.'

"'In blindness, Jasper?'

"'There's the wind on the heath, brother; if I only feel that, I would gladly live for ever. Dosta, we'll now go to the tents and put on the gloves; and I'll try to make you feel what a sweet thing it is to be alive, brother!'"

You may search literature through for the like of this matchless dialogue, which in half a page sums up the character of both speakers—the anxious, foreboding, melancholy questioner; the merry answerer with his pagan creed and *joie de vivre*. Borrow is always sketching this Petolengro for us, always by the same method of question and answer that is so quaintly effective :—

"'. . . We are not miserable, brother,' says Petolengro.

"'Well, then, you ought to be, Jasper; have you an inch of ground of your own? Are you of the least use? Are you not

Stones from a Glass House

spoken ill of by everybody? What's a gipsy?'

"'What's the bird noising yonder, brother?'

"'The bird? Oh, that's the cuckoo tolling; but what has the cuckoo to do with the matter?'

"'We'll see, brother; what's the cuckoo?'

"'What is it? You know as much about it as myself, Jasper.'

"'Isn't it a kind of roguish, chaffing bird, brother?'

"'I believe it is, Jasper.'

"'Nobody knows whence it comes, brother?'

"'I believe not, Jasper.'

"'Very poor, brother, not a nest of its own?'

"'So they say, Jasper.'

"'With every person's bad word, brother?'

"'Yes, Jasper, every person is mocking it.'

"'Tolerably merry, brother?'

"'Yes, tolerably merry, Jasper.'

George Borrow

"'No use at all, brother?'

"'None whatever, Jasper.'

"'You would be glad to get rid of the cuckoos, brother?'

"'Why, not exactly, Jasper; the cuckoo is a pleasant, funny bird, and its presence and voice give a great charm to the green trees and fields. No, I can't say I wish exactly to get rid of the cuckoo.'

"'Well, brother, what's a Romany chal?'

"'You must answer that question yourself, Jasper.'

"'A roguish, chaffing fellow, ain't he, brother?'

"'Ay, ay, Jasper.'

"'No use at all, brother?'

"'I see what you're after, Jasper.'" ...

So the pages run, in their audacious newness of method that is Borrow's own invention, and his alone; it is happily impossible to copy, for how tired we should get of indifferently done Borrow! He does not confine himself, however, to two or three principal characters in his

Stones from a Glass House

books; there are hundreds of tiny character-sketches dropped in, as it were, in spite of himself:—

"I met the other day an old man who asked me to drink. 'I am not thirsty,' said I, 'and will not drink with you.'

"'Yes, you will,' said the old man, 'for I am this day one hundred years old; and you will never again have an opportunity of drinking the health of a man on his hundredth birthday.'

"So I broke my word and drank.

"'Yours is a wonderful age,' said I.

"'It is a long time to look back upon,' said the old man; 'yet, upon the whole, I am not sorry to have lived it all.'

"'How have you passed your time?' said I.

"'As well as I could,' said the old man; 'always enjoying a good thing when it came honestly within my reach—not forgetting to thank God for putting it there.'

"'I suppose you were fond of a glass of good ale when you were young?'

George Borrow

"'Yes,' said the old man, 'I was; and so, thank God, I am still,' and he drank off a glass of ale."

This is the sort of thing the books are full of, though Petolengro, Isopel Berners, Mrs. Herne, and the Flaming Tinman are the principal characters that are woven into a sort of plot through *Lavengro* and *Romany Rye*. Isopel is the heroine, so to speak, of these books (which are not novels, though they have a hero and heroine), Borrow being always his own hero. Isopel appears suddenly in *Lavengro*—comes driving her donkey-cart into the dingle where Borrow had camped, and there she sees him through his fight with the Flaming Tinman, and then she pitches her tent beside him, and we are aware that the heroine has come upon the stage at last. But Isopel drifts out of the book just as she came into it, and even Dr. Knapp cannot reveal to us why she came and why she went, and whether she and

Stones from a Glass House

Borrow ever met again. The *Life* assures us that every line Borrow wrote was autobiographical, and that all his characters are drawn strictly from life. Well, they may be; but they have a curiously convenient way of expressing Borrow's own peculiar prejudices, as, for instance, his unaccountable hatred against Sir Walter Scott. It is not likely that two different wayfarers ("the man in black" and the Hungarian) should have expressed Borrow's views on this particular subject as they did.

I am inclined to think that Borrow often invented a character just for the purpose of airing some of his pet ideas through the mouthpiece of a new personage, else, as I have said, their views would not have so often agreed with his own. *Lavengro* and *Romany Rye* were written long after the wanderings were over, when Borrow's views on all subjects had been formed, and he expresses them frequently in these

George Borrow

books; indeed, it is one of the uses of the *Life* that after reading it one is able so easily to pick out which are Borrow's views in his writings and which are the genuine utterances of his characters. Borrow's views are, alas! just what one should skip in *Lavengro* and *Romany Rye:* railings against Popery, railings against Sir Walter Scott, railings against publishers and critics—these are the spots upon his feast of charity.

It was at the end of the wanderings which are described in *Lavengro* that Borrow started on his continental journeyings, and got his appointment at St. Petersburg to translate the Bible into Mandschu-Tartar. This occupied his energies for several years, from 1830 to about 1834–35, when he was engaged by the Bible Society as their agent for distributing Bibles in Spain. It may be extremely uncharitable to say so, but the Bible Society surely engaged a curiously

Stones from a Glass House

unsuitable agent for their work! What is termed "the missionary spirit" was not exactly characteristic of George Borrow. *The Bible in Spain* tells all about what he did on those travels for Protestantism; but good reading as the book is, and ardent as its author appears to be in the cause he has espoused, there is an undeniable ring of falsity through the book. The whole enterprise was manifestly undertaken by Borrow purely in the spirit of adventure and to make a living for himself; while it was demanded of the Bible Society's agent that, in his reports, zeal for the Protestant faith alone should seem to have been his aim when he began the work. So, like everything written to order, *The Bible in Spain* fails in spontaneity. The adventures, indeed, are written with gusto, and there are enough of them to carry off the woeful cant which fills in between scene and scene; but throughout Borrow was pur-

George Borrow

sued by the idea that he was writing for the Bible Society, and was ever artist in direr strait? There is something exquisitely ridiculous in the whole situation—the plight of Borrow, the plight of the Bible Society—it is hard to say which of the two must have been more bewildered. The story goes that "*there always was a large attendance* in the Society's rooms" on the days when Borrow's letters were to be read, and one can believe it. But story does not relate whether, in Spain, Borrow sat puzzling over how to dish up his adventures with the proper seasoning of zeal, and, I dare say, wrote many a line "with his tongue in his cheek," as the vulgar saying goes. Now, this may be doing Borrow an injustice, but it is certainly the impression which one gets in reading *The Bible in Spain*, and to read between the lines is often the best way of getting the truth out of a book. Nothing, it is true, could

Stones from a Glass House

outdo Borrow's hatred of Popery, and he rushed at this part of his mission with a perfect fury of zeal; but a hatred of Roman Catholicism is quite a different matter from the love of righteousness, which alone can justify "missions" of any kind whatever; and the distribution of Bibles should surely be undertaken out of a spirit of love, not out of a spirit of hatred! All this, however, did not seem to strike the reading public, and *The Bible in Spain* remains to this day far the most popular of Borrow's books. Perhaps the religiosity of its phrases actually pleased a large section of the public; more probably the truth is that the class of readers who "sell a book" are just those who are incapable of appreciating the best things of literature, and positively prefer the second best in art. *Lavengro* has never reached the same popularity as *The Bible in Spain*, and it never will, just because it is much better literature.

George Borrow

The last years of Borrow's life are sad to read of. Though his money difficulties were at an end after he married and his books became successful, he seemed to create troubles for himself in a curious way. He was always rushing into controversies with his critics and quarrels with his friends in the most unnecessary manner. A gloom and disquiet hang over these last years; we lay down the *Life*, wishing that we had not been told about them, and agreeing with Herrick that the poet's poetry should be his pillar. We prefer to forget now that Borrow ever lived to be a quarrelsome, egotistical old man, vain of very shallow acquirements which he immensely overestimated as immortal contributions to the science of philology; and try to think of him as the romantic wanderer with a "winning tongue" that charmed men's secrets out of them, with gallant bearing and dauntless courage, and all the manly virtues rolled together.

Stones from a Glass House

Happily this is the picture that the books conjure up when the *Life* is not at hand for reference, so it will remain as the permanent portrait in the days to come. All poor Borrow's philology (they say) has been superseded by the more exact and scientific methods of this drearily precise generation; some one else has written much more reliable "facts" about gipsies, quite unadorned by imagination and entirely true; his translations from many tongues are unread, and I doubt if all the Bibles he strewed so industriously over the Spanish Peninsula did very much against the Faith he hated; but when the chaff of his life's work is winnowed away there remains a goodly quantity of wheat upon the threshing-floor. Three delightful books at least remain, which will charm many and many a generation of readers—as solid a contribution to literature this, as most writers can hope to make.

"AS COMPARED WITH EXCELLENCE"

THE present state of book-reviewing is extremely unsatisfactory. Never, in the history of literature, have books received so much attention at the hands of critics as they do just now; yet, with it all, neither the public nor the authors have reason to be satisfied with the results of all this so-called critical writing. It is hard to say which suffer most—the authors who are injured by injudicious reviewing, or the public which is taught to read the wrong books; but one thing is certain, that both are grievously sinned against.

Criticism, from being practised by the few and competent, has become a trade carried on by the many and singularly unfit. Every paper, however obscure, has

Stones from a Glass House

its "literary" column, and Heaven alone knows who the writers of these columns are—they are frequently much more illiterate than their readers. But it is not the decline of criticism as an art that is the deplorable feature of the case—for even the best and highest criticism is, after all, uncreative work such as the world can do without—it is more the disastrous effects of all this loose, fatuous criticism that we regret. These effects, as I have said above, are traceable both in the writers and in their public; and the first and most glaring defect in modern criticism is its tendency to over-praise. To spoil our authors by injudicious praise is quite as bad as, if not worse than, crushing or trying to crush them by over-severity; in either case the goose that lays golden eggs for a greedy public may be killed; there is, however, a refinement of cruelty in the modern method of author-murder decidedly reminiscent of the butt of Malmsey. In

As Compared with Excellence

past times we heard a great deal of the old slashing reviews (the historic review which "killed Keats" being an obvious example); but few people, perhaps, take into sober consideration how many budding Keats have been killed by kindness—a fully quicker form of murder than the older method. Let any careful observer of the literary history of the last ten or fifteen years search back in his memory and see if he cannot remember a score of authors who have come by their literary death in this way. We all know the steps of this tragedy: the first clever book, received with an outburst of intemperate praise, *from critics whose trade it is to over-praise*—then the quickly growing "boom" in this particular author's books; the more and more slovenly work appearing year by year, the unpruned style confirming in all its vices till what was at first a mere accident becomes a vicious mannerism—and then cometh the end. For

Stones from a Glass House

swift is the descent into the literary Avernus. Is it too much to say that many and many of these pitiful disasters are caused only by indiscreet criticism—or, rather, want of criticism?

The moment that hundreds of critics tell a young writer that he has practically nothing to learn, that his art is perfect, his style mature, and so on, he will in nine cases out of ten believe their pleasant voices; he stops all effort, trusts to this "genius" with which he finds himself credited on every side, and dashes on down that steep path which it is all but impossible to reascend. You will say that the man is a fool who believes all the pleasant things that are said about him; but human nature being what it is man will always believe smooth prophecies, and can scarcely be blamed for doing so. The blame in such cases rests entirely with the false prophets, and it is at their hands that the blood of the author will be required.

As Compared with Excellence

If great kindliness of heart, a dread of hurting others, a desire to encourage talent —if these were the springs of such criticism it would be more possible to condone it. But it is scarcely possible to believe that this is the case, and the sordid reasons for fatuous reviews must be plainly stated. In the first place it may be cynically observed that the majority of present-day reviewers bear ever in mind the Scriptural truth, *The merciful shall obtain mercy*—most of them write books themselves, and wish to be "done by" as they "do unto others." Therefore it behoves them to praise the work of their fellow book-and-review-writers, be that work what it may—their own time is coming, their own bread and butter may depend upon it—and what do truth and art matter where it is a question of bread and butter? (Alas, too true!)

This is not, therefore, so bad as that purely commercial side of reviewing which makes the critic review a first book from

Stones from a Glass House

a promising author with his eye, so to speak, upon the second book from the same pen. Let me explain, for the benefit of the innocent, the full working of this scheme.

The real merit of a book has, unfortunately, comparatively little to do with its selling properties—the really important thing is that an author's name should be well known. Once a name is established, the publisher is sure of getting a certain number of thousands of copies of each book sold, no matter what trash it may be. Obviously, then, the first duty of conscientious tradesmen in books is to get up a boom about the author he wishes to sell.

Now, of course, no amount of praise will ever do this unless the book has some intrinsic merit to recommend it; so the critics and the publishers must select for their victim a promising author. If this be done, and the book has sufficient merit to justify some of the praise bestowed upon

As Compared with Excellence

it, the boom should be easy to work. The first book having been so widely written about, the second by the same author receives even more attention from the public, and after this the mysterious "name" is made and sales are assured—for a term of years—till the public get tired of so much of the same fare and will have no more of it.

This is no new accusation against critics and publishers—readers of Macaulay will remember his delicious tirade on this subject in 1830:—

"It is time [he writes] to make a stand against this new trickery. The puffing of books is now so shamelessly and so successfully carried on that it is the duty of all who are anxious for the purity of the national taste to join in discountenancing the practice. All the pens that were ever employed in magnifying Bish's lucky office, Packwood's razor strops, and Rowland's Kalydor seem to have taken service with

Stones from a Glass House

the poets and novelists of this generation.

A butcher of the higher class disdains to ticket his meat; we expect some reserve, some decent pride in our hatter and our bootmaker. But no artifice by which notoriety can be obtained is thought too abject for a man of letters. It is amusing to think over the history of most of the publications which have had a run during the last four years—*the publisher is often the publisher of some periodical work.* In this the first flourish of trumpets is sounded —the peal is then echoed by all the other periodical works over which the publisher or the author, or the author's coterie, may have any influence. At present we too often see a writer attempting to obtain literary fame as Shakespeare's usurper obtains sovereignty. The publisher plays Buckingham to the author's Richard. Some few creatures of the conspiracy are dexterously disposed here and there in the crowd. *It is the business of these hirelings to throw up their caps and clap their hands and utter their ' vivas.'*"

As Compared with Excellence

This plain speaking on Macaulay's part did as much good as plain speaking generally does. Seventy years have passed since these words were written, and yet the same system goes on—certain periodicals praise, and will always praise, all the publications of certain houses; there seems to be an occult connection between them which cannot be denied. Even from a commercial point of view this system is a mistake; for the simple reason that it generally, in time, ruins the authors which it attempts to establish. One of the great objects of those who get up a boom in the work of any special writer, is to get the unfortunate man to repeat himself as much as possible: " When will Mr. —— give us another idyll of —— shire?" "We hope it will not be long before Mrs. —— paints another picture of life in her village—we want more country-folk of the type of Jess and Jem," &c. " Miss —— is at her best in depicting London society,

Stones from a Glass House

we look forward eagerly to her next." . . . And so on.

Why all this eagerness for similarity? Are the critics aware that self-repetition is a fault—that variety of range, diversity of subject, freshness of treatment, are the very blood and bones of live literature? It would seem that they are not, if we may judge by their strenuous appeals to authors to stick, each man, to the "vein" in which he has made his first success. Of course, these appeals fall upon a deaf ear where the writer is strong enough to be uninfluenced by his first reviews; but the point I am arguing just now is the case of the young author, and the case of the author talented, perhaps, but without genius. A sad list might be made out of what Stevenson called "pretty reputations" which have been ruined by the attempt to repeat a success. The history of literature produces few examples of successfully repeated success—the vast

As Compared with Excellence

majority of attempts in this kind being dismal failures. Of course, it is natural that we should wish more from an author who has delighted us; but we should recognise that we do not want the identical characters dished up a second time, but new characters—the newer the better, and treated as freshly as may be, the only sameness required being the describing mind. Let us by all means encourage our favourite writers by wanting more from them, but not "more of the same" —remembering the sadly wise Persian proverb, "No man can bathe in the same river twice."

Diversity of subject is, alas! the last quality that the tradesmen of literature wish, because *it is similarity that sells*— for a few years. "Why do you suppose my second book did not please the public as well as my first?" asked a discouraged young novelist of a wise friend.

"Because it was not exactly the same,"

Stones from a Glass House

was the reply. "Your first was about a drunken mother and two sons; so the public would have liked your next to be about a drunken father and two daughters."

It may be objected here that it is hard if the public may not get what they like; but the fact of the matter is that the public will like almost anything they are told to like. And this is where the immense responsibility of reviewing comes in. So widespread is the influence of the press just now, that I suppose not one person in a thousand chooses his own books without having heard of them through some newspaper or magazine. This is quite natural, and, in the present state of the bookworld, reviews form an indispensable bridge between the writer and the reader. But this only makes it more necessary that reviews should be trustworthy, for if the blind lead the blind we know that both will fall into the ditch. There is no

As Compared with Excellence

ditch the public is more apt to fall into than this of the boomed book.

"One reads about it everywhere" is the reason commonly given for getting certain books; and few readers take the trouble to inquire *why* they see this special book noticed everywhere—they simply take the assurance of excellence upon trust, their taste is formed for them by the consensus of opinion. "There must be something in it," one has often heard the bewildered yet trusting reader exclaim. "There must be something in it, all the reviews praise it." At first, perhaps, a struggle goes on in the mind of the more intelligent reader: he questions whether the book is really as fine as it is said to be; then the iteration of its praises takes effect as iteration generally does, and he comes to believe in merits which native sense would have led him to disclaim.

This great, childish, trusting public is the principal sufferer from unwise review-

Stones from a Glass House

ing. They read mainly the reviews in daily papers and in the cheaper magazines, and these, for obvious reasons, are the organs which publish the most ignorant and fatuous notices of books. For the old-established reviews and magazines do not sin after this manner to anything like the same extent as their cheaper brethren.

The uneducated public have a profound respect for anything in print. The reviewer is to them a sort of Jove, and at his nod they obey, spending their time and their money on the books he recommends.

One evening some months ago I travelled out to the suburbs of London in a crowded third-class carriage. Two mechanics sat beside me, elderly, tired-out looking men, black with work. The moment they got into the train they began to speak about books—those few books they managed to gulp in the spare moments going to and from their work.

As Compared with Excellence

Books seemed to be their glimpse into Paradise, the way they mentioned the titles of each work was something to hear. But ah! the books they mentioned!

"What are you *studying* now, Jake?" said one. "*I* am *mastering* —— by ——" (naming one of the most popular and most trashy books of the day).

The other replied with such pitiful pride that I could have wept for him: "Oh, I am *studying* —— by ——." His choice was, if possible, worse than that of his companion. Till the train stopped they both sat reading away at their worthless books as earnestly as if their salvation depended upon it.

The reviewers who teach an ignorant public to reverence such trash are as guilty as the quacks who persuade their victims to buy worthless drugs—perhaps more guilty. Here were two men, intelligent, thirsty for mental stimulus, and instead of reading Scott, Dickens, Thackeray

Stones from a Glass House

—aye, or Kipling or Thomas Hardy—they were spending all their poor leisure on books which could supply them with neither help, instruction, nor amusement; the newspapers had told them that these were marvels of literature, therefore they read them and thought, or tried to think, that they enjoyed them—that was all.

It is a deplorable state of matters if these reviewers are more or less suborned to write what they do not honestly believe about books; but it is perhaps fully more deplorable if they do believe what they write—if, in short, they are as incapable as they seem to be of knowing a good book from a bad one. Dr. Johnson in one of his inimitable sentences gave what might serve as a touchstone for all criticism. When asked his opinion upon a book of verses by a young poetess, he replied: " For a young lady's verses good enough —*as compared with excellence*, nothing."

Could criticism be at once fairer or

As Compared with Excellence

more searching? He gives the young lady her due of praise, yet keeps steadily before him her entire failure when compared with the classics. This "comparison with excellence" is not enough practised in our generation. It is indeed the fairest, most genuine test by which to try every new-comer in the field of literature. You will perhaps say that it is too searching a test—that modern books cannot stand comparison with classics and live; but this is not the case. The best modern books stand the test perfectly, it is only the second best that fall before it. And this is exactly where the uses of comparison come in—to help us to distinguish between the first and the second rate in art. There should be, in fact, a standard of art in the mind of every real critic by which we can measure the stature of each applicant for fame. If, for instance, the enthusiastic first critics of the "Kailyard" school of Scottish fiction had,

Stones from a Glass House

before writing their reviews, read over a few of the incomparable cottage scenes in *The Antiquary*, these would surely have suggested searching comparisons between the old and the new schools of Scottish fiction, and a few of the superlatives would have been erased from the reviews. Or if, again, the eulogists of the new pseudo-historical romances had taken half-an-hour of *Esmond*, before composing their eulogies, they would surely have gained an almost painful insight into all that the new historical writers are not.

But this wholesome system of comparison has gone quite out of fashion just now—in the mind of our modern reviewers no distinctions of literary rank seem to exist. Now the majority of our novel writers are only society entertainers of greater or less ability; quite an honourable calling if recognised for what it is and followed frankly for what it can "bring in." But it is a confusion of terms to speak of such men

As Compared with Excellence

and women as belonging to the same profession as Fielding, Scott, Thackeray, or Jane Austen. The reviewers, however, if we may judge from the expressions they employ to describe each new book, decide to ignore this great and fixed gulf which separates the artist from the tradesman. I select at random from a publisher's advertisement some criticisms upon a new historical novel; this is what the reviewers have to say about it · "It is sublime—*there is nothing else like it in literature.*" "It is one of the greatest historical novels that has ever been written . . . one of the greatest historical novels of the world." I have not read the work in question; but, without undue scepticism, I fancy it would be possible to find its counterpart in literature. Eulogies of this kind defeat their own end, and are quite enough to make intelligent people decide not to read the book; moreover, no self-respecting author could bear to see

Stones from a Glass House

his work written about in this way, for he must know that it can only bring down ridicule upon it. Moderate praise, temperate adjectives, a degree of fault-finding, and a sympathetic appreciation for what is attempted as well as what is accomplished, these are the signs of the true critic.

The question of fault-finding is, of course, a delicate one; but there can never be anything like a school of criticism without it. To their fearless system of fault-finding the *Edinburgh Review* critics owed their fame.

"Jeffrey's reviews [says a writer in the *North British Review*] were all parts of a great and gradually matured system of criticism, and the object aimed at in by far the greatest proportion of the essays, was not so much to produce a pleasing or attractive or interesting piece of writing, as to enforce great principles of thought, to scourge error and bigotry and dulness, to instil into the public mind a just sense

As Compared with Excellence

of the essential requisites of taste and truth in literature, and to dispense and wear away by constant energy that crust of false sentiment which obscured and nearly extinguished the genius of this country at the commencement of the eighteenth century."

This was indeed a huge undertaking—to cure a diseased public taste and teach it new standards of truth and beauty. But Jeffrey set himself to the task unflinchingly. His system of criticism was terribly severe—hence its fame. But he could praise quite as heartily as he could censure. If you will glance over his reviews of the Waverley Novels, for instance, you will be struck at once by the fearless way in which he mixes praise and blame. No modern critic would dare to point out their faults to any of our popular novelists as Jeffrey points out the faults of *The Monastery* and *The Abbot* to Sir Walter :—

Stones from a Glass House

" They are certainly the least meritorious of the whole series [he says], and while they are decidedly worse than the other works of the same author, we are not sure we can say, as we have done of his *other failures* [how calm !], that they are better than those of any other recent writer of fiction. *So conspicuous, indeed, was their inferiority*, that we at one time apprehended that we should have been called upon to interfere and admonish the author of the hazard to which he was exposing his fame. But as he has since redeemed that slip we shall pass it over lightly, and merely mention one or two things that still live in our remembrance. . . . The euphuist, Sir Piercie Shapton, is *a mere nuisance throughout*, nor can we remember any incident in an unsuccessful farce more utterly *absurd and pitiable* than the remembrance of tailorship that is supposed to be conjured up in the mind of this chivalrous person, by the presentment of the fairy's bodkin to his eyes."

In the same way Jeffrey chastises Galt ·

As Compared with Excellence

" His next publication is undoubtedly the worst of the whole—we allude to *the thing* (!) called *The Steamboat*, which has really no merit at all . . . with the exception of some trash about the Coronation which nobody, of course, could ever look at three months after the thing itself was over; it consists of a series of *vulgar stories*, with little either of probability or originality to recommend them," &c.

I have quoted these two examples of Jeffrey's criticism because they were both directed against popular authors of the day, and therefore exhibit the fearless, impersonal attitude which the reviewer then took up compared with the attitude of the modern critic towards the favourites of the hour If a writer is popular just now, it is not too much to say that he may write (and publish) what he chooses, secure of receiving nothing but praise for it. This is not criticism in the real sense of the word; and I believe that every

Stones from a Glass House

good writer, if asked his opinion, would vote in favour of more truly *critical* reviewing. For the true critic is the author's best friend. To ask for this kind of criticism is not to ask for vindictive, slashing reviews, but for more grave consideration, more helpful suggestion. Reviewers have two snares laid ready for their unwary feet : they are apt either to hail some new-comer who is not a genius as if he were one ; or they entirely fail to discern genius when they encounter it. Needless to say that the former is our specially modern snare, while the latter was that of the older school of reviewers.

Jeffrey, a sound, impartial critic in most cases, could not do justice to such an entirely new writer as Wordsworth, and his name will be associated for all time with the fatal dictum, " This will never do," with which he prefaced the review of *The Excursion. New greatness* is, of course, difficult to judge, because it conforms to

As Compared with Excellence

no standards and seems to glory in defying all known rules of art, making new rules for itself. But this cannot excuse any man who named himself a critic for committing such a mistake as Jeffrey made in his reviews of Wordsworth. It is true that he asserted " Nobody can be more disposed to do justice to Mr. Wordsworth's great powers than we are," but with the same breath he held up Wordsworth's whole poetical system to ridicule. Ridicule of an elaborate, slow-going kind was a great weapon in those days. *The Excursion* is analysed canto by canto, almost line by line, with sarcastic comments added. The whole spirit of the great poem in this way eluded the critic, only the letter remained. It seemed impossible to Jeffrey to ignore the weak points of these poems; he must emphasise them so much that their far greater beauties were obscured in the process.

Stones from a Glass House

The White Doe of Rylstone was the subject of his peculiar ridicule :—

" This we think," he says, " has the merit of being the worst poem we ever saw printed in a quarto volume It seems to consist of a happy union of all the faults, without any of the beauties, which belong to his school of poetry. . . . In the *Lyrical Ballads* Mr. Wordsworth was exhibited, on the whole, in a very pretty deliration; but in the poem before us he appears in a state of low and maudlin imbecility, which would not have misbecome Martin Silence himself, at the close of a social day."

Yet this severe critic is roused to enthusiasm by the poems of Thomas Campbell: "There are but two noble sorts of poetry, the pathetic and the sublime; and we think he has given very extraordinary proofs of his talents for both," he says. For Felicia Hemans he has only praise. There is "the very spirit of poetry" in the

As Compared with Excellence

"bright and vague picturings" of one poem and "a fine and stately solemnity" in another. "There would be no end," he admits, "to our extracts if we were to yield to the temptation of noting down every beautiful passage which arrests us here."

These extracts from the critical studies of Jeffrey exhibit very clearly this difficulty, which all reviewers labour under, of appreciating the entirely new manifestations of genius. Poor forgotten Campbell and Felicia Hemans were in Jeffrey's day new writers, but not new thinkers—they expressed the same thoughts that all the other poets of their kind were used to express, in the same sort of language—therefore they were admired. But Wordsworth appeared, a writer who had broken fresh ground in the fields of thought and expression. Both his ideas and the form in which he expressed them were entirely novel—he had parted company from the

Stones from a Glass House

past and all its traditions. There was no one to compare him with, and Jeffrey, bewildered by this, went astray in his criticism of the new poet.

Now, it may be objected, that it is just at this crucial point—the right of judging of *new greatness*—that the system of " comparison with excellence " breaks down, because such greatness owes its existence to its divorce from those past models that you would compare it with. But this is not the case. It is always possible to compare the *scope* of a new writer with that of his predecessors, however widely separated the form in which he finds expression may be from the models of other days. Does he touch life at as many points as they did? Is he as true to nature as they were? It is on these things and not on the perpetually changing element of form that a writer's claim to greatness must eventually rest. And until the critics realise this, that a book

As Compared with Excellence

with small ideas cannot be great, and that greatness must be sought for in the constitution of a book, its essential ideas not till then will reviewing be other than it is.

MODERN TRAGEDY

THE average reader will always tell the librarian of his circulating library that he wishes a book with a happy ending; he will, in extreme cases, even return every volume which cannot be recommended as "coming right in the end" with the emphatic remark that he never reads unhappy books. The fact is that he likes, and quite rightly, to read a description of what life should be, rather than of what it really is; he resents the more truthful picture.

But literature worthy of the name cannot be made to order; and the best writers are no more affected by the protests of thousands of average readers than the incoming tide might be. The author who deliberately caters for his audience must be content to be classed as a tradesman

Modern Tragedy

only, and must renounce the title of author without a murmur.

So it follows that in spite of the demand for cheerful books, the bias of literature is towards tragedy. This can be easily accounted for. Books—again let me add worthy of the name—are written by men who think, and to thoughtful men life must always seem very sad—hence the sad books.

By a sort of apostolic succession, the literature of tragedy which began long ago with the first story-tellers has descended to our own times, changing in form from generation to generation, yet keeping its distinctive note unmistakably through every phase of treatment. For the great tragic subjects cannot alter—man's fate, man's struggles, man's doom; these, the very roots of tragedy, can suffer no change.

But true as this is, it is curious to notice how differently the old subjects

Stones from a Glass House

are handled by each generation. I say generation instead of writer, because the writer is only the utterer of the thought of his times; he is formed by it, and gives synthetic expression to the conclusions of thousands of other men who have thoughts but no words. Now from time to time curious waves of change pass over the thought of men. These waves of change seem sudden to the careless onlooker, but are really the result of very slow processes. After what we may call a "thought wave" has washed over a generation, it will be found to be viewing, from an entirely new standpoint, the identical problems which exercised the preceding generation. The problems of life which form the subject of all tragedies cannot, as I have said, alter; but our way of viewing them may suffer extraordinary changes. I wish, if possible, to show the differences in our modern view of tragedy.

And first of all, what is tragedy?

Modern Tragedy

It is (says the dictionary) "*a species of drama in which the action and language are elevated and the catastrophe sad.*" But for the purpose of this article it may be very simply defined as a presentation, whether in the form of drama or novel, of the dark, unexplainable side of human things.

Every son of Adam has, at one time or another, questioned the cause or the meaning of his own sorrows; but before the tragic sense which produces a great tragic writer can arise, this questioning spirit must be turned away from a man's individual miseries and focussed on the woes of the world. For to attain to the first rank of tragic writers it is not enough that a man should suffer and then reproduce in literature his own torments; but it is absolutely necessary that he should have so entered into the sorrows of the race, as to be able to create types of each grief which he writes about. You will quickly

Stones from a Glass House

see that no one individual experience can ever be universal enough to include the griefs of the whole world, yet that insight may supply the lacking knowledge. This insight for grief not his own is the very hall-mark of tragic writing—it is the tragic sense, and is the possession only of the best writers. Shakespeare, for instance, has so much of the tragic insight that he can write as convincingly of Lady Macbeth's remorse as if he had himself committed murder and shuddered over his guilt.

The possession of this tragic sense, then, opens the eyes of certain men in each generation to see more clearly than their fellows the grievous side of existence, and this clearness of vision leads them to all manner of questionings. It is in the answering of these that ancient and modern tragedy first sharply divide, for the main contention of ancient tragedy was that the ills of life were sent

Modern Tragedy

us from the gods, while the great object of modern tragedy is to show that these evils are the inevitable outcome of natural laws, and that thus we are very often the authors of our own miseries. Examples of the old and new methods will perhaps make this point more clear.

As a typical instance of the ancient tragic method, let us take the world-known tragedy of Œdipus. It is, as all men know, the story of a cursëd race. A curse rested on this house; it was prophesied that Œdipus was to kill his father, and though, to falsify the prediction, the boy is separated from his parents and grows up a stranger to them he cannot escape his fate. So he meets his father all unawares, fights with him and kills him. Then farther to fulfil his dark destiny, Œdipus returns to his kingdom, meets his mother Jocasta without knowing who she is, marries her and becomes the father of her children. Then the

Stones from a Glass House

curse is fulfilled, but it descends with the same relentless force upon the innocent children of the unnatural marriage—their tragic lives and deaths are chronicled in the other plays of the series.

Now what is the meaning of all this ghastly story? It is to present the great riddle of the Universe in dramatic form: the undeniable, horrible fact that a curse, a fate, a destiny—what you will, rests on men; that a tremendous Power, not themselves, is always either warring against them or working for them. And what, according to Sophocles, is Destiny —this moulder of men's lives? It is the will of God—or rather, in the speech of these times, of the gods.

Behind this mystery he cannot penetrate: why the gods turn men to destruction he does not know, unless it be "for guilt of old." There is a note of uncertainty even in this explanation when Œdipus speaks of–

Modern Tragedy

> "Sad calamities
> Which I poor wretch against my will endured,
> For thus it pleased the gods, incensed, perhaps,
> Against my father's house for guilt of old."

It seems indeed, as Dronke points out. that Sophocles wishes only to exhibit this profound mystery of divine overruling in the affairs of men without making any attempt to explain it. Darkness is all around man's path by his showing:—

> "Ah, race of mortal men
> How as a thing of naught
> I count ye, though ye live!
> For who is there of men
> That more of blessing knows,
> Than just a little while
> To seem to prosper well
> And having seemed to fall?
> With thee as pattern given,
> Thy destiny, even thine, ill-fated Œdipus,
> I count naught human blest."

Œdipus is to Sophocles typic of the human race :—

> "Search where thou wilt, thou ne'er shalt find a man
> With strength to 'scape when God shall lead him on,"

Stones from a Glass House

he says, and the whole meaning of the tragedy is to be found in these words. The puzzle is, to discover why God leads man as he does into darkness and not into light. If you wish to illustrate anything, you will always do so more forcibly by taking an extreme instance for your illustration; and Sophocles acted on this principle when he chose the story of Œdipus as an illustration of the terrible workings of that power which we name Destiny.

By a series of all but impossible contingencies, the characters of the play are brought into the desired situation—than which nothing more ghastly could be imagined. This is the method uniformly followed in ancient tragedy. The old plays are full of these violent, frightful situations, undreamed of by modern writers. No weak concession is made here to the happy ending preference of readers—for when in the hands of master

Modern Tragedy

writers, readers must learn to take what is given them. With that inspiration for the truth of art which we seem almost to have lost just now, the older tragic writers recognised that genuine tragedy must begin as it is to end, and end as it had begun. The modern trick of trying to let a ray of light in upon the scene at the end was unknown with them. Their plots are ghastly beyond description—a cataclysm of horrors gathered round the doomed man who is to illustrate the dark ways of Fate—he is made to marry his own mother, eat his own children, or some such horrible impossibility. But to create these situations it is necessary that the writer should make a personality of Destiny; that he should, as it were, see this power deliberately moving the pawns on the chessboard of life at its will. This is what the old writers wrote to prove; and it is exactly what the modern mind hesitates to admit. For two quite im-

Stones from a Glass House

personal powers are now supposed to be the arbiters of our poor fortunes—these are Circumstance and Heredity. With these impersonal powers there can be *no possibility of intervention*, and their conviction has robbed many of our modern tragedies of much dramatic flavour. In the older drama there was always at least the possibility that Destiny might be appeased—that man might struggle and supplicate, perhaps even wring from this power that moved the world some mitigation of his agonies. But to pray to Circumstance would indeed be futile, and to entreat the great ghost Heredity vainer still—so the modern drama looks for no surprises. We are, in fact, becoming too great slaves to probability, with a corresponding loss on the dramatic side.

As a perhaps rather glaring instance of modern tragic methods which are directly opposed to the ancient tradition, Ibsen's *Ghosts* may be selected. Here is the plot:—

Modern Tragedy

Oswald, the hero, comes home in bad health to his mother's house. In the first act the reader has been told that Oswald's father has led a dissipated life, but Mrs. Aveling has always concealed this fact from her son. The boy returns to tell his mother the terrible verdict of a doctor who attended him when he was ill—his constitution is hereditarily tainted and he will go from bad to worse. He has decided that should his former symptoms return he must end his life, and he explains this to his mother in a scene of horrible power.

"*O.* 'You must come to the rescue, mother.'
Mrs. A. 'I!'
O. 'Who is nearer to it than you?'
Mrs. A. 'I, your mother!'
O. 'For that very reason.'
Mrs. A. 'I who gave you life.'
O. '*I never asked you for life. And what sort of a life have you given*

Stones from a Glass House

me? I won't have it, you shall take it back.'"

The poor mother is in despair—she sees the truth of his words, yet shrinks from the act which he urges. The play ends at the moment when Mrs. Aveling has to make her decision. Oswald is, as the doctors prophesied, stricken at last. His wits gone, he sits stupidly in his chair begging for "the Sun, the Sun." The reader is left in doubt as to whether Mrs. Aveling does or does not kill her afflicted child. Well, here is tragedy indeed, of the most piercing quality; but you will notice the extremely modern note which is struck throughout. This is no tragedy of God's making: it is the work of man. The whole mechanism of the tragedy is dissected before us· "This is how misery is manufactured," Ibsen seems to say, and with professional calm he exhibits the process to us. There is no veiled figure

Modern Tragedy

of Destiny in the background here, no pressure of circumstance; the whole situation is quite easily and plainly accounted for by the gross selfishness of the parents who thought only of their own gratification and forgot the child who might have to bear the burden of inherited diseases. What in olden time would have been attributed to the gods is now entirely attributed to man. Æschylus in the *Agamemnon* asks:—

> " What with mortal man
> Is wrought apart from Zeus,
> *What of all this is not by God decreed?*"

And Ibsen would boldly answer, " Much of it." He has little patience for the man who would (so to speak) make God responsible for his sins.

Ibsen is, in short, more of a moralist than an artist. Certain ideas possess him like a mania—the inevitableness of character, man's incapacity to escape from himself, and the huge burdens laid upon the

Stones from a Glass House

innocent by the guilty. These ideas have not only taken possession of Ibsen, but of our whole generation, and too much brooding over them had produced another very marked development among our writers, *i.e.* the over-estimation of heredity as a factor in tragedy.

"Here," they say, "we have at last discovered the very root of tragedy." And this discovery has done a great deal to ruin their art. In their eagerness for truth they have sacrificed truth itself and art along with it. For, as Huxley said, "In ultimate analysis everything is incomprehensible": you may, that is to say, be the cause of your child's temperament, but what caused your own, and that of your father, and his father—and so on *ad infinitum?* You may force the inquiry back and back till it ends always in the utter incomprehensibility of first causes. Character, in short, is something quite beyond explanation, except in a very

Modern Tragedy

limited sense. Its real mystery is unassailable.

And by trying to do away with this mystery and "explain" everything, modern tragic writers have degraded their art more than they have any idea of. This failure of the modern method may be illustrated very fairly by trying to apply it to any of the Shakespearian tragedies. Thus: Try to trace the madness of Lear to natural causes; analyse the unnatural natures of his two eldest daughters, trace it to a species of "alienism," inherited perhaps from Lear himself, whose mental condition must always have been unsound or it would not have broken down even under all the weight of his troubles. Conjecture how Cordelia came by her more normal mental equipment, trace it to a sounder physique, or show how she inherited it from a normal mother, or speculate as to whether she was a reversion to some far-off ancestor;

Stones from a Glass House

account, in fact, for the whole tissue and being of the great tragedy, and where is it? It has disappeared altogether, and only a laughable travesty of the alienist's note-book remains.

The same process may be applied to any of Shakespeare's plays with the same dire result. Trick up the sublime ardours of Antony and Cleopatra in modern dress, and you have only a study of the erotic temperament in woman, together with an analysis of the frailty of man more or less disgusting. The whole spectacular splendour of life is destroyed by these analytical methods; just as (to use a hackneyed but good metaphor) you destroy the beauty of a flower by picking it to pieces. It is true that the botanist knows more about the flower after this process of destruction; but for purposes of beauty we all prefer our rose entire. A great play, or novel, should not be a contribution to Science, but to Art, and in

Modern Tragedy

forgetting this truth how many have erred! But unfortunately the scientific spirit is creeping more and more into our literature,—it is so much in the air just now that apparently writers have to inhale it like the influenza microbe. Everything must be analysed—the ingredients of character like the components of our food—accounted for, explained, either by Heredity or Circumstance.

The tragedy of Circumstance has its ablest exponent in Mr. Thomas Hardy. Unlike Novalis, who held that Character was Fate, Mr. Hardy seems to maintain that Circumstance is Fate. This is the answer he gives to the old agonised questions—the same questions that tormented Sophocles and Æschylus, and will torment all thinking men till the world ends.

Tess of the D'Urbervilles and *Jude the Obscure* are both studies in Destiny—tremendous arraignments of the "well-

Stones from a Glass House

judged plan of things and their ill-judged execution." Every one knows the story of Tess. She is the sport of Circumstance from her cradle to the gallows on which she ends her life; time and again the moment comes for some Unseen intervention, and nothing intervenes; at each crisis of her story Circumstance hounds her forward to destruction. When she is betrayed by D'Urberville there is no Eye to pity, no Hand to save.

"Where was Tess's guardian angel?" our author asks. "Where was Providence? Perhaps, like that other god of whom the ironical Tishbite spoke, he was talking, or he was pursuing, or he was in a journey, or peradventure he was sleeping and was not to be awaked."

And again he defines his view of things :—

"Nature does not often say, 'See!' to her poor creature at a time when seeing can lead to happy doing; or reply,

Modern Tragedy

'Here!' to the body's cry of 'Where?' till the hide-and-seek has become an irksome outworn game. We may wonder whether at the acme and summit of the human progress these anachronisms will become corrected by a finer intuition, a closer interaction of the social machinery than that which now jolts us round and along; *but such completeness is not to be prophesied or conceived as possible.*"

We are, in short, says Mr. Thomas Hardy, caught all of us in the wheels of the clumsy machine of Circumstance, to be "jolted around and along" at its unintelligent will. This seems to be the peculiar problem which Mr. Hardy has set himself to solve, or rather to illustrate— that thinking, reasoning creatures should be made the sport of unreasoning laws. He has worked out one aspect of the problem in *Jude the Obscure.*

Jude is a man of bright intelligence and keen sensitiveness. Born a working man,

Stones from a Glass House

he has all the ambitions of a scholar, but this is not where the tragedy comes in. Poor Jude is the predestined fool of his passions as well as of his circumstances. He marries, miserably, the first woman who attracts him, and the story of their degraded intercourse is meant to typify the whole tragedy of sex.

He meets, too late, his true love, Sue Bridehead, and there follows on this all the matrimonial confusions which have made the book a by-word. Jude and Arabella, and Sue and Sue's husband, become almost laughably mixed up in the plot, till it emerges again into unmistakable tragedy at the close. The author has never lost sight of the end, though the reader may have done so, and he has been working up to the climax like all good writers. Jude has been divorced from Arabella, and married to Sue by this time, and they have two children; they

Modern Tragedy

have also living with them Jude's child by his former marriage with Arabella.

"The boy's face expressed the whole tale of his situation. On that little shape had converged all the inauspiciousness and shadow which had darkened the first union of Jude, and all the accidents, mistakes, fears and errors of the last. He was their nodal point, their focus, their expression in a single term. For the rashness of these parents he had groaned; for their ill-assortment he had quaked; for their misfortune he had died."

Oppressed by the thought that "there are too menny of us," the boy hangs himself and the other two children, and thus rounds off as it were the misfortune of his existence. But Jude's miseries have still to culminate. Sue leaves him, in a fit of frantic repentance after the death of her children, and he is once more ensnared by the gross Arabella. Stupid

Stones from a Glass House

with grief and fuddled with drink, he returns to her, and at the same time renounces the will to live. He is dead before death, crushed by the pressure of laws which he cannot understand or fight against—great primal laws which urged him on and then left him to destruction. When at last the curtain falls on Jude as he lies stark under the sheet, " straight as an arrow, the thumping that had gone on in his breast for nigh thirty years stopped at last," we feel tragedy could not go much further. The book gives expression to the despairing thought of a whole doubting generation, which hesitates to name life a boon. The Accuser stands forth, and challenges with no uncertain voice, who dares and can to answer his charges. Look, he seems to say, at this man, this creature of a few unhappy years —with his aspirations of a God and his instincts of a beast! If an Individual Power made this ill-contrived toy, such

Modern Tragedy

a Power must be either foolish or merciless; if impersonal Forces alone were at work, how shall we regard the process? —as an ugly joke to be laughed at with a wry face, or a calamity to be faced as best we may and endured as long as we will?

It is not difficult to make out which of these views Mr. Hardy inclines to, and his influence may be traced through the great mass of modern tragical fiction—man the sport of Circumstance, the fool of his own nature; these themes are worked out with every possible variation by hundreds of minor writers who have the mistaken idea that by handling a big problem they write a big book. They would do well to content themselves with smaller questions and leave Mr. Hardy to grapple alone with these weighty matters. These tragedies of Circumstance are peculiarly depressing to consider; because, as I have pointed out, there is no possibility of intervention

Stones from a Glass House

between a man and his fate if there is no deity save Circumstance behind things—if, in fact, Circumstance is Fate. As good examples of this view of life, the novels of Mr. George Gissing may be considered. It is impossible to find more deadly depressing books; circumstance, *probable* circumstance, is to him everything. No matter what a man is, he will be overborne by the force of Circumstance and moulded to its shape. It matters more to a man, according to Mr. Gissing, whether he is born rich or poor than whether he is born wise or foolish, good or bad. The gallant old tales of man the conqueror, wresting from a life the most inauspicious all the gifts of fortune — these traditions of a credulous age are swept away like cobwebs by Mr. Gissing. Life and Circumstance are here the conquerors of man, who lies passive under their blows. What is to become of us if we adopt this view of life? Surely a larger, saner outlook is possible, and we

Modern Tragedy

may see that a power greater than itself is behind Circumstance.

All the different tragedies—ancient and modern alike—which we have considered, have involved a problem; but there is another form of tragedy, and that the highest, which involves no question but is content simply to express the darkest side of human affairs. This is the Shakespearian method. The agonised questioning of man's destiny so characteristic of ancient tragedy is absent here · God is not, so to speak, called to account for the sorry happenings of life. Neither is Circumstance omnipotent, nor Heredity, after the modern tradition. But the characters, without any intervention of the author or any explanations of any kind, explain themselves and their situation. The result of this simplicity of method is the consummate, matchless tragic note never struck before or since by any other writer. An illusion of reality is produced by it

Stones from a Glass House

which can never be attained to by our modern scientific methods which research into character for generations back, and show each man the product of his conditions.

By none of these methods, but by the exercise of a tragic sense the most perfect possible, Shakespeare produced his incomparable tragedies. Certain of his scenes stab one to the heart exactly as the sight or hearing of such a scene in real life would do; and this because, rejecting the ancient tragic tradition which depended for its effectiveness upon situation alone, Shakespeare's tragic sense unerringly recognised that the passions of humanity were the beginning and end of the tragedies of the world:—

> "In tragic life, God wot,
> No villain need be
> Passions spin the plot,"

as George Meredith puts it. That is to say, a life may be one long tragedy, and

Modern Tragedy

yet have no tragic "situations" in the ancient sense. It is true that Shakespeare's tragedies always have a tragic plot, but you will notice that *the plot is not, as in ancient tragedy, the meaning of the play:* it is quite subordinate to the characters. Shakespeare does not wish to tell a tragic story—he wishes to describe men and women at a crisis of emotion. Here the old and new join hands instead of parting company. Nothing is more congenial to the modern tragic writer than the description of tragedies of character. The fear is that nowadays this vein will be overworked. Shakespeare chose the great passions of the human heart for his character studies : Remorse — Cruelty— Ambition—Love or Hate ; but some of our modern writers find the minor passions quite worthy of study. In this kind are the tender little tragedies of Jane Barlow and Mary Wilkins—chronicles for tiny griefs—petty sorrows—pitiful little disap-

Stones from a Glass House

pointments—calamities of mice. These tales seem to exhibit the morbid sensitiveness of the modern mind, which makes so much out of little—sees tragedy everywhere.

The tragic sense, in fact, seems to be wearing rather thin with the lapse of the centuries, and there is a want of the old robustness of view among us. Like a river lost among sands, the stream of literature is being broken up into thousands of rivulets and is losing the force of a current. Instead of one or two great writers who can, by giving their opinions, really contribute to public thought, we have crowds of minor authors whose opinions are of no weight, all confusing public thought by their strife of words. Each has his own tiny tragic vein—the tragedy of want, or of intemperance, or disease, or lunacy—their numbers are endless: great subjects all of them, if greatly handled; but that is

Modern Tragedy

seldom done. The tragedies of drunkenness alone would stock a library; but where is the epic among them all? It is seldom that one opens a modern novel without coming across some painful description of mania in its many forms—yet again, where is the classic among them? One cannot help wondering why this should be the case; why, when a whole generation of writers is evidently keenly alive to the tragic side of life, there should yet be no great tragic writers among them —saving always Mr. Thomas Hardy.

Is there enough of *acknowledged mystery* in our modern work? Enough of the great, vague, infinite background which you find in ancient and Shakespearian tragedy—a background of the unexplained, the unknowable—the never to be explained or known on this side the grave?

"THE OTHER GRACE"

"Add but *the other grace—be good—*
 Why want what the angels vaunt."—BROWNING.

FASHIONS in clothes : fashions in manners : fashions in speech, and fashions in heroines: the law finds no exception.

The general idea of how a book comes to be written is, that the author is possessed by certain characters and incidents and has no rest until he has described them ; it would be better for literature if it were so. But only to the past masters in the craft belongs this glory of creation ; the great mass of writers do not create—have, that is to say, no independent conception of their characters ; they merely wait until the masters have clearly created a new type, then they take possession of that type whatever it may be, dress it up anew,

"The Other Grace"

place it in fresh surroundings, and try to pass it off as a novel creation of their own.

The masters have indeed, in this way, a good deal to answer for; just as the High Priest of Fashion is answerable for a good deal when he thoughtlessly sends every woman in Europe into crinoline or large sleeves, as the case may be. A Zola, for instance, or a Hardy, astonishes the world with a splendid, if brutal, bit of work. The public fancy is fascinated by the type. "*We must paint life as we see it, nothing like life! passion! virility!*" cries every literary dabbler; and forthwith begins to try this style of painting. "*We can all do it, nothing easier!*" they say—and it is astonishing how long they take to tire of these attempts. Long after the reading public has become completely sated with a certain class of book, these imitative writers are persistently producing it, seized apparently with a curious blindness,

Stones from a Glass House

which keeps them from seeing that they are doing the thing that has been done perhaps a hundred times already. At last, however, there comes a breathing space. What will they be at next? asks the anxious reader, scanning the literary horizon for a sail, so to speak. Perhaps it is a Stevenson this time who comes like Hopeful to give a hand out of the Slough of Despond. His style is lucid, his types are clearly defined—again "*nothing easier*," is the cry. In a trice the imitators are tricked out in doublet and hose to follow their leader, and the historical romance runs merrily on its way. Then, just as something new is wanted, comes—let us say, a Barrie. Ah, what fresh fields, what pastures new! But they are not long uninvaded. "Whence came their feet into my field and why?" he might rather appropriately inquire, for the green fields are getting all trodden and tashed nowadays. It is so easy to write about old

"The Other Grace"

mothers, and dominies, and ingle-neuks and the Shorter Catechism! One might multiply examples indefinitely. I have merely chosen these at random to illustrate what every intelligent reader must have noticed — that there is fashion in books, as in so many other things.

The master-minds are responsible for the type of hero or heroine which is for the nonce to reign in public favour; and it is a curious fact that since first novels began to be written, *heroines* have been divided into far more marked types than heroes. I do not pretend to account for this fact; but I think that it is one. The earlier novelists bestowed all their powers of characterisation upon their male characters: there was plenty of individuality in them; but they seemed to be contented with one fixed type of heroine—the then ideal of woman—and added her as a sort of stage property to every book. Fielding, in Sophia Western, describes the type

Stones from a Glass House

which reigned triumphantly for many a day :—

"I never heard anything of pertness, or what is called repartee, out of her mouth; no pretence to wit, much less to that kind of wisdom the affectation of which in a young woman is as absurd as any of the affectations of an ape. No dictatorial sentiments, no judicial opinions, no profound criticisms. Whenever I have seen her in the company of men she hath been all attention, with the modesty of a learner, not the forwardness of a teacher. . . . I once, to try her only, desired her opinion on a point which was controverted between Mr. Thawckum and Mr. Square. To which she answered, 'You will pardon me. I am sure you cannot in earnest think me capable of deciding any point in which such gentlemen disagree.'"

Such was Sophia : and she may be recognised in almost every one of Scott's heroines, and survives even in Thackeray's

"The Other Grace"

Amelia Sedley — the "gentle creature" who "took her opinions from those who surrounded her, such fidelity being much too humble-minded to think for itself."

But the Sophias and Amelias of the past are indeed dead and done with now, and a new type of heroine has arisen and now rules despotically over the whole world of fiction. The new type may be divided into two classes of favourites: the Outcast woman, and those whom, for want of a better name, I shall call the Sirens; and everywhere we read of "pure women," whose special claim to that title seems to be their lack of purity.

The sad fact is that "good women," in the plain Saxon meaning of the words, are gone out of fashion—in books at least—and until the tide of public opinion turns, we must submit to the reign of her successor as best we may.

This statement that good women have gone out of fashion will probably be re-

Stones from a Glass House

ceived by many people with a shriek of protest; for it is quite one of the worst features of the Siren that she masquerades as an angel.

The idea has got abroad that, provided the heart is pure, the intention harmless, nothing is wrong, and the Siren is continually acting in the most unprincipled way with the best intentions in the world. But let us examine these two types of modern heroines more closely.

Two famous heroines of the Outcast order—*Tess* and *Trilby*—belong to a type now crystallised in the public imagination. And to exhibit the nobility that lies in every one, however degraded, is now the favourite *motif* of the day. Heaven forbid we should deny the possibility of such good; but the thing may be carried a little too far, and it is coming to this nowadays, that such women are depicted as being capable of more generous action, more heroic impulse than their worthier

"The Other Grace"

sisters. The worst of the whole business is that no one can breathe a word against this new morality but the word Pharisee is whispered, and that dubious legend of Christ and the Magdalene adduced for argument. Moreover, so great is the cry for charity just now, that it would be considered woeful harshness in any writer to describe a woman of scandalous antecedents without dowering her with such traits of nobility and generosity as wipe out the stain of sin, and melt the reader to tears of sympathy. We are becoming too lax altogether: the stern old rule "hate the sin and love the sinner" is being forgotten, and we are asked to condone the sin till there remains no more hatred of it, nor any looking for of judgment upon it. Charity is a lovely grace; but sentimentality is a weak vice. Let us take care that the one does not lapse into the other. There may be here and there in the curious annals of the human race a

Stones from a Glass House

Tess or a *Trilby*—but the most charitable must admit that they are exceptions, and only prove the rule that a bad life is a tolerably clear proof of a bad heart. This is a fact there is very little use in denying, though for the purposes of making interesting character-studies the novelists are fond of doing so.

These heroines of avowedly bad character yet redeemed by traits of nobility are, however, less dangerous favourites for the public fancy than the all-conquering Siren; for the good reason that they are such manifest creations of the imagination that very few people set much store by them—they like to read about them and wonder if they are possible characters, but they are doubtful, and possibly disapproving all the time. The Siren, on the contrary, seems to have fairly possessed the British imagination—it is scarcely possible to open a novel in which she does not appear. The Siren is a creature of wild

"The Other Grace"

unrestrained passions, desperate, unscrupulous, emotional yet heartless, incapable of sound judgment or of self-control, and quite without all womanly feeling. She is, in fact, a most repulsive character, yet we are asked to find her irresistible, a very Queen of Hearts to whom the whole male creation bend the knee in wonder and admiration. Now, no one doubts the reality of this character: who has not met a Siren?—they are all too common. But the curious thing is why we should be asked to admire her? Her morality is of such a hopelessly involved order—submitting as it does to none of the recognised moral codes—that we follow her devious relations with the sterner sex in disgusted perplexity. She has always (alas for him!) a husband, for the unmated heroine is as extinct as the Dodo; then she is involved in intricate connections with some other woman's husband; there is also the man who should have

Stones from a Glass House

been her husband, and there is always the husband of her soul, sometimes even the second husband—a very carnival of husbands—till we are fain to ask the Sadducee's question, *Whose wife shall she be at the Resurrection,* &c. &c. &c. ?

This is the creature round whose character a myth as unsubstantial as vapour is being raised just now. Only she, we are told, can "taste the colour of life"—less ardent natures are poor, and of necessity lead lives of foolish emptiness; only the passionate Siren is capable of the greater heroisms: passion holds the field; and the woman who does not exhibit this eminently feminine grace is not held to be worth writing about. There is no doubt that the Siren makes an effective figure in fiction; but what of the truth of the presentation? A fire of straw throws out a prodigious glare, yet who would "watch a winter's night" beside it?

None of the authors who with such

"The Other Grace"

enthralling art have painted these pictures of outcast women—take *Tess* and *Trilby* once again as instances—none of them ever continued the picture. Their heroines were invariably doomed to death, because the art-insight capable of limning a Tess or a Trilby at the white-heat of passion knew too well to try to paint the impossible—Tess or Trilby trudging through life with the object of her ardours.

But, perhaps because her history has not often been recorded by masters of the craft, the Siren is not handled with this consistency. She is the darling of the scribbler, for her type is now so clearly defined that she is very easy to manage. She is shown to us in all her fervour, living at a white-heat as great as ever Tess or Trilby went through; but instead of being consistently killed off, we are actually asked to believe that she lives on after the story closes. Imagination

Stones from a Glass House

does not conjure up a very pleasant picture of the Siren's later years. She would, unless we are much mistaken, exhibit none of the charms of old age; try to fancy her at threescore and ten, her beauty (which is always described as of the "alluring" type) gone; her many lovers grown cold in consequence; left alone with all her exotic passions burnt out, and her heart like a heap of ashes. Impossible that in her long pilgrimage she has gained the respect of any human being; she has no female friends, for the good reason that she thought no woman worth making friends with in the days of her youth; the husband she long ago deserted for another man, not unnaturally has nothing to do with her now, while the "other man" has also proved faithless; the children she neglected can scarcely be blamed for neglecting her in their turn; and the curiously unexacting Deity whom she was supposed to worship,

"The Other Grace"

has vanished long ago into that limbo where the False Gods dwell.

This would be the inevitable age following upon a youth such as the Siren is supposed to lead. For we are not always young, and the lust of the eyes and the pride of life pass away like a dream, and with them there passes away every quality upon which this modern heroine depends for her charm. It is extraordinary if all the accumulated experience of all the centuries has taught us no more than this, and if we can possibly bring ourselves to accept this exotic erotic creature as a heroic type of all that woman should be —if, indeed, we can bring ourselves to imagine that she has any heroic qualities whatever. No heroine, in the brave old significance of the word, was ever made of this stuff: which of us in age or weakness would lean on this broken reed?

I am no stickler for subject—let who will write about what he pleases, however

Stones from a Glass House

unpleasant, so long as he writes truly ; and the Siren, a type all too common in life, might well be common in books also, if she were only described as what she is, instead of as what she is not. In art, a " study " is valuable only as it is truthful ; and something of the same holds good in literature. But there is one study often set to beginners in art—to paint white objects against a white background, and the tyro is clever indeed who gives them form and substance and yet retains the whiteness : white souls too are hard to paint, but will some clever painters not essay the task for very love of its difficulty?

WALT WHITMAN

"CAMERADO," says Walt Whitman in his envoi to *Leaves of Grass*, "this is no book—who touches this touches a man"; and would-be students of the remarkable utterances known to fame as the poems of Walt Whitman should remember this, the author's own estimate of his book. "Most of the great poets are impersonal," he said again when questioned about his writings. "I am personal; they portray their endless characters, events, passions, love-plots, but seldom or never mention themselves. In my poems all concentrates in, radiates from, revolves round myself. I have but one central figure, *the general human personality typified in myself.* Only I am sure my book inevitably necessitates that the reader transpose him or herself into

Stones from a Glass House

that central position, and become the actor, experiencer, himself or herself, of every page, every aspiration, every line."

Thus in Whitman's poems one must look both for the portrait of the man himself, and for his portrait of Man in the abstract as he conceived of him—"the general human personality" that Whitman saw "typified in himself"—and in neither instance will the portrait be uninteresting.

Here is a huge personality—repulsive in some aspects, lovable in others; and it is bared to us with a frankness of pre sentment that cannot fail to hold our attention. We may not be able to discern his charm—we may see only his horrid attributes, but we have met in these three hundred and eighty pages which make up *Leaves of Grass* a new character of extraordinary force.

Only a proper understanding of this character will make us understand the poems, and only a real knowledge of the

Walt Whitman

poems will make us form a true estimate of the character; so the two are one and indivisible and must be studied together.

Although a large number of people read at the present time, it is really a very uncommon thing to find an author studied in a serious way. We read after an easy fashion, singling out for praise or for blame short passages from books and letting the author stand or fall by these. We look, in fact, to the particular, not to the general; and few of us can give any reasonable account of why we admire such or such an author. Yet to grasp the central idea of a book is surely the only intelligent way in which to read it: to find out *what made the writer write his book*, should be the aim of every reader.

Now Walt Whitman has suffered more serious misconceptions from idle and casual readers than almost any other author. His poems are picked at in detail, quoted piecemeal, and made easy fun of just be-

Stones from a Glass House

cause very few people take pains to find out what they are really about. There is nothing easier than to make fun of these poems ("pieces," as Whitman himself called them), and it takes close study to understand or to appreciate them. For the artist's gift of making his meaning quite unmistakable has been denied to our author; he always has an idea in everything that he writes, yet to get at what that idea is, is often exceedingly difficult just from his contempt of the mere technicalities of art. But it is not for lovely verses or pleasing rhymes that we are to look here, but for Ideas—and these we shall find in plenty if we take the trouble to search for them.

Leaves of Grass, Whitman's volume of poems, is not a random collection of verse; it is a book of structural design, a planned and connected series of poems to illustrate certain theories. The first edition of this remarkable book appeared in 1855, but for

Walt Whitman

eight years before this date the poems had been planned, and it took Whitman nearly thirty years to perfect his conception in the final edition of 1881. In this time much was rewritten, much destroyed altogether, yet the main conception remained unaltered from the first.

"My underlying purpose in these poems was religious," Whitman says—a statement which will surprise the casual reader mightily. For at first sight these poems seem to be of the earth earthy, and to deal not at all with the things of the soul; how then does their author profess to write "religiously"? I think the best way to show this is to let him speak for himself, as he does in hundreds of lines. The essentially spiritual nature of matter is the main idea which runs through and through *Leaves of Grass.* This is the key to the cypher of Whitman : this is his religion ; or perhaps, more truly, it is the foundation upon which his religion is built :—

Stones from a Glass House

"I will not make a poem" (he says),
 "or the least part of a poem, but has reference to the soul,
Because, having looked at the universe, I find there is no one, nor any particle of one,
But has reference to the soul.
I will make the poems of materials,
For I think they are the most spiritual poems."

And again he says:—

"Strange and hard that paradox true I give,
Objects gross and the unseen soul are one."

Utterances like these throw a flash of light over the whole of the book; this then is the meaning of the apparently meaningless lists and enumerations that fill up the pages! His eye can rest on no object, let it be never so unsightly or foul, but he must sing its praise because he sees "the soul" in it. No wonder that his

Walt Whitman

muse is prolific! He does not need to wait for "inspiration": everything is an inspiration, and must be sung about straightway. Hence Whitman's method —so peculiarly his own—of running on for pages at a time in this sort of vein :—

> "House-building, measuring, sawing the boards,
> Blacksmithing, glass-blowing, nail-making,
> Coopering, tin-roofing, shingle-dressing,
> Ship-joining, dock-building, fish-curing, flagging of side-walks by flaggers,
> The pump, the pile-driver, the derrick, the coal-kiln," &c. &c. &c.

All these enumerations are really meant to make Whitman's meaning plain to his reader, though they have in nine cases out of ten the opposite effect. He will not credit his reader with intelligence enough to see that the word "all" necessarily includes everything, and so to emphasise

Stones from a Glass House

his theory he goes into ridiculous detail of what he means "all" to include.

I will not pretend to deny that one must laugh at this method of Whitman's, nor to assert that a better method might not have been found. What must be said for it is that it is his own, and that it seems to express the man's rugged, uncompromising nature better than any more polished method could have done.

If you can only keep steadily in mind that what Whitman is wishing to preach to you is *the Spirit underlying materials*, his whole writings will at once become plain to you, and you will see how each of his doctrines have a connection with the other In this way: Because of the Spirit that underlies all material things humanity is sacred, and because humanity is sacred it has great potentialities; therefore self-fulfilment is a supreme virtue; and in self-fulfilment lies the great hope of the Ideal Democracy—also in the

Walt Whitman

spiritual nature of man Whitman bases his hopes for immortality. These, then, are the main ideas to be searched for :—

(1) The Spirit underlying all materials.
(2) The potentialities of our nature.
(3) Self-fulfilment.
(4) Democratic ideals.
(5) The good end of all.

The possibilities dormant in every human being are sung by Whitman with a force and conviction that carry us along with the singer :—

> " The man's body is sacred and the woman's body is sacred,
> No matter who it is, it is sacred. Is it the meanest one in the labourers' gang?
> Is it one of the dull-faced immigrants just landed on the wharf?
> Each one belongs here or anywhere, just as much as the well-off, just as much as you,
> Each has his or her place in the procession.

Stones from a Glass House

A man's body at auction (for before the war I often go to the slave market to watch the sale).
I help the auctioneer—the sloven does not half know his business!
Gentlemen, look on this wonder!
Whatever the bids of the bidder they cannot be high enough for it,
For it the globe lay preparing quintillions of years without one animal or plant,
In this head the all-baffling brain,
In it and below it the making of heroes,
This is not only one man, this the father of those who shall be fathers in their turns,
In him the start of populous states and rich republics, of him countless immortal lives . . .
How do you know who shall come from his offspring through the centuries?"

Again and again we have this lesson repeated to us in different words:—

Walt Whitman

"We consider bibles and religions divine.
I do not say they are not divine,
I say they have grown out of you, and may grow out of you still,
It is not they who give the life, it is you who give the life,
Leaves are not more shed from the trees, or trees from the earth, than they are shed out of you."

Here we have Whitman at his best—ridiculous no longer, but the preacher of a robust and inspiring creed which we would all be well to take to heart. I call Whitman's creed "robust" because it is reasoned out, and is the logical outcome of his belief in the spiritual nature of the universe; it is not the rootless optimism which vaguely sees good in every one without having any sufficient reason for doing so. He sees good in every person because he thinks all the universe is good:—

"I am myself just as much evil as good,

Stones from a Glass House

> and my nation is—*and I say there is in fact no evil (or if there is I say it is just as important to you, to the land, or to me, as anything else)*. ...
> I will show that there is no imperfection in the present, and can be none in the future,
> And I will show that whatever happens to anybody, it may be turned to beautiful results,
> And I will show that nothing can happen more beautiful than death,
> And I will thread through my poems that time and events are compact,
> And that all the things of the universe are perfect miracles, each as profound as any."

> "Why should I wish to see God better than this day?
> I see something of God each hour of the twenty-four, and each moment then,
> In the faces of men and women I see God, and in my own face in the glass,

Walt Whitman

I find letters from God dropt in the streets, and every one is signed by God's name,
And I leave them where they are, for I know that wheresoe'er I go,
Others will punctually come for ever and ever."

Seeing God (or good) in all things, Whitman scarcely admits evil as a real existence; for "*it is important,*" he argues, and what is "important" cannot rightly be named evil. Every man, however seemingly vile, "has his part in the procession"; we must accept life as a whole, not seeking to find fault with any part of it.

Pursuing this doctrine Whitman launches out upon a dangerous voyage and comes to shipwreck. In that section of *Leaves of Grass* which he names "Children of Adam," the attempt is made to show in detail that nothing is common or unclean. These unfortunate chants instead of accomplishing their end have defeated it, but they

Stones from a Glass House

remain as extraordinary human documents. That a man should be found to sing these songs out of an honest and good heart, as Whitman certainly sang them, is a curious freak of individuality. It is as though a man should assert his right to walk among his fellows naked and unashamed. To call Whitman impure, obscene, and many other ugly words, is to misunderstand him altogether; he is only asserting the creed he believes to the uttermost, with no thought or caring for the opinion of the world. He will show a stupid public that "every creature of God is good," and should be accepted with thanksgiving. Here the strong self-poised individuality of the man appears. At the first appearance of *Leaves of Grass* such a tempest of popular abuse fell upon Whitman as would have silenced almost any other man for ever. Not the style of the book, but the morals of its author were attacked with extraordinary bitterness. And what

Walt Whitman

does the author do? "I went off," he says, "to the east end of Long Island and spent the late summer there—*the happiest of my life*—then came back to New York with the confirmed resolution, from which I never afterwards wavered, to go on with my poetic enterprise in my own way, and finish it as well as I could!" Later, when he was offered favourable terms for another edition of his book if he would consent to leave out a few lines from two of the pieces, he refused to do so. "I dare not do it," he said; "I dare not leave out or alter what is so genuine, so indispensable, so lofty, so pure."

With something of the spirit of a fanatic he pursued his way, heedless of either public opinion or the remonstrances of friends. Even the advice of Emerson—at that time the very god of American idolatry—was disregarded. "For something like two hours," we are told, Emerson argued with him on the subject of those

Stones from a Glass House

verses collectively known as *Children of Adam*. Whitman tells the story of this interview in the *Critic* for December 1881 :—

"Up and down this breadth of Beacon Street, between these same old elms, I walked for two hours of a bright, sharp February midday twenty-one years ago, with Emerson, then in his prime, keen, physically and morally magnetic, armed at every point, and, when he chose, wielding the emotional just as well as the intellectual. During these two hours he was the talker, and I the listener. It was an argument, statement, reconnoitring, review, attack, and pressing home (like any army corps in order, artillery, cavalry, infantry) of all that could be said against the part (and main part) in the construction of my poems, *Children of Adam*. More precious than gold to me that dissertation (I only wish I had it now verbatim). It afforded me ever after this strange and paradoxical lesson : each point of Emerson's statement was unanswerable, no judge's charge ever more complete or

Walt Whitman

convincing—I could never hear the points better put—and then *I felt down in my soul the clear and unmistakable conviction to disobey all, and pursue my own way.* 'What have you to say then to such things?' said Emerson, pausing in conclusion. 'Only that while I can't answer them at all, I feel more settled than ever to adhere to my own theory and exemplify it,' was my candid reply. Whereupon we went and had a good dinner at the American House. . . "

And there can be no doubt that Whitman had the right of the matter. The author who will change the whole conception of his book to suit the taste of any other man is a poor creature, and does not deserve to be remembered by posterity; and Whitman was man enough, and artist enough, to trust his own inspiration.

Sincere admirers of Whitman's poems must always regret that by the publication of *Children of Adam* he brought his other

Stones from a Glass House

and nobler poems into discredit, yet they must also recognise that Whitman had no other course open to him. He had conceived the idea of the book as a whole, and to leave out this section would have been to maim it. The pity is that the conception included as much as it did. The reader must be referred to the original here, for, unfortunately, *Children of Adam* cannot be quoted. It is, as Thoreau wrote in a severe yet appreciative letter—" It is as if the beasts spoke." These utterances, however, must be read by any one who wishes to understand either Whitman or his philosophy. Here his theories are pushed to their utmost conclusion, with the result that he will probably be misunderstood as long as he is remembered at all. The reading public have a fatal, though perhaps natural, way of fastening upon and remembering the weak or the nasty bits of a book. *Children of Adam*, undeniably Whitman's weak

Walt Whitman

spot, will always be quoted against him. Those who admire our author in spite of his aberrations from sane taste, must accept this portion of his book for what it is worth—a human document far more valuable from its frankness of self-revelation than for the doctrines which it professes to teach.

But the special interest which attaches to this section of *Leaves of Grass* is the fact that the whole after-tragedy of Whitman's life was involved in his determination to publish these verses. Poetry is never a lucrative trade; but in Whitman's case his poems had more than a negative influence on his career. After the close of the war, in which he had, as a helper to the wounded, played such a splendid part, Whitman was appointed to a clerkship in the Department of the Interior, but he had only held this position for a short time when he received his dismissal "because he was the author of *Leaves of*

Stones from a Glass House

Grass." Another appointment was obtained for him before very long, so the material loss was not so great as it seemed to be at first; but the slur upon his moral fame remained, and the case roused such discussion for and against the poems that Whitman found himself involved in unenviable notoriety. The questionable portions of the book were canvassed and quoted to the detriment of all that was noble and beautiful in it, and new readers were found for it just because they were curious to read such mysteriously objectionable verses. With far too much of the partisan spirit Whitman's few genuine admirers rushed to his defence. That turgid bit of pamphleteering, " The Good Grey Poet " of Mr. D. O'Connor, is a case in point; the hot-headed author has no words bad enough for Whitman's detractors, none good enough for Whitman himself—" Shakespeare, Homer, Æschylus, Dante, Isaiah—his place is beside these

Walt Whitman

bards of the last ascent, the brothers of the radiant summit." Now, over-praise is fully more injurious to an author's reputation than over-blame, and to place Whitman on the radiant summit with Shakespeare and Isaiah is only to call down ridicule upon him; so between friends and foes it went hard with poor Whitman and his *Leaves of Grass* about the year 1865. Still new editions of the unfortunate book kept struggling out in an intermittent way, and always in unexpurgated form, that testified to the author's inflexible determination to publish what he himself approved. Each "edition," so called, was really an expansion of the former edition, and contained some new section of the poet's first conception. The various editions up to 1882, when the book was really completed, cover a period of nearly thirty years, and the story of the book is the story of its author. He was so identified with his work that he seemed

Stones from a Glass House

to have no life apart from it, for all his experiences to him were embodiments of theories. The earlier and the mid-period poems are one long chant of the joy of existence :—

> "Beginning my studies the first step pleased me so much,
> The mere fact consciousness, these forms, the power of motion,
> The least insect or animal, the senses, eyesight, love,
> The first step I say awed me and pleased me so much,
> I have hardly gone and hardly wished to go any further,
> But stop and loiter all the time to sing it in ecstatic songs."

This is only the prelude to his ecstasies. "*Each moment and whatever happens thrills me with joy,*" he says further, and then following his own curious method, he will go on to explain all the different things—whether experiences of mind or of

Walt Whitman

body—that cause his joy. All these recitations are peculiarly " Whitmanish," if one may coin a word: they are the very essence of his art such as it is, and in them he exemplifies his great theory of Democratic art. In plain words, his theory amounts to this, that the true artist of the future must not go far afield for his subjects; or as he puts it:—

> " The hourly routine of your own or any man's life, the shop, yard, store, or factory,
> These show all near you by day and night—workman! whoever you are, your daily life!
> In that and them the heft of the heaviest —in that and them far more than you estimated (and far less also),
> In them realities for you and me, in them poems for you and me, ... in them all themes, hints, possibilities.
> I do not affirm that what you see beyond is futile,
> I do not advise you to stop,

Stones from a Glass House

I do not say leadings you thought great are not great,
But I say that none lead to greater than these lead to.
Will you seek afar off? You surely come back at last,
In things best known to you finding the best, or as good as the best,
In folks nearest to you finding the sweetest, strongest, lovingest, . . .
The popular tastes and employments taking precedence in poems."

Whitman becomes very amusing in his enthusiastic preaching of this doctrine; for not only does he contend that the homeliest themes are the best, but he finds a good deal to say against other and more classic subjects :—

"Come, muse" (he cries), "migrate from Greece and Ionia,
Cross out, please, those immensely overpaid accounts,
That matter of Troy and Achilles'

Walt Whitman

wrath, and Æneas', Odysseus' wanderings,
Placard 'Removed' and 'To Let' on the rocks of your snowy Parnassus,
Repeat at Jerusalem, place the notice high on Jaffa's gate and on Mount Moriah,
The same on the walls of your German, French, and Spanish castles, and Italian collections,
For know a fresher, busier sphere, a wide, untried domain awaits, demands you!"

He then tells us (by the old enumerating method) of the places now deserted by the muse : of the vanished traditions of Romance—the Crusaders streams of shadowy midnight troops sped with the sunrise, Arthur vanished with his knights—dissolved like an exhalation—"*passed! passed! for us for ever passed that once so mighty world, now void, inanimate, phantom world,*" and breaks out into an ecs-

Stones from a Glass House

tatic vision of the future pathway of the muse (!):—

> "I say I see, my friends, if you do not, the illustrious emigré
> Making directly for this rendezvous, vigorously clearing a path for herself through the confusion,
> By thud of machinery and shrill steam-whistle undismayed,
> Bluffed not a bit by drain-pipes, gasometers, artificial fertilisers,
> *Smiling and pleased with palpable intent to stay,*
> *She's here, installed amid the kitchen ware!*"

This is just the same doctrine which Kipling sang thirty years later when he assured us that "Romance brought up the 9.15" (train); and there are elements of great truth in the doctrine. It is in fact wholesome fare for those who can assimilate it—some of us cannot do so; and without any question it is well to be able

Walt Whitman

to take this view of things in a world that becomes yearly uglier and uglier.

Mr. Symonds, in his illuminating study of Walt Whitman, remarks that "there is a danger lest the solution of this problem should suffer from being approached too consciously," and the truth of this prophecy, written some eight or ten years ago, must be apparent to all careful readers of modern fiction. There is far too much conscious struggle after "simplicity" of theme, "primitive" subject, and so on—too much "installing of the muse among the kitchen ware" in fact; as if the selection of simple subjects will ever produce simplicity of treatment when the author himself has the complex, introspective, self-conscious modern mind.

But I wander from my point. Whitman was not self-conscious in his selection of subject. To him these present-day matters were the subjects of subjects;

Stones from a Glass House

most genuine he was in his announcement of their wonder and beauty. If you consider that many of these poems were written forty-five years ago, you will be surprised at the modernity of them; for we are inclined to consider this theory of the beauty of ugliness as entirely a doctrine of our own day. In this, as in many other respects, Whitman was before his time; there can be no doubt that *Leaves of Grass* would have been received more calmly nowadays than it was in 1853; its beauties would have been more quickly appreciated, and its blemishes would not have created such an uproar. Whitman himself wrote :—

"You who celebrate bygones,
Who have explored the outward, the surfaces of the races, the life that has exhibited itself,
Who have treated of man as the creature of politics, aggregates, rulers, and priests;

Walt Whitman

I, habitan of the Alleghanies, treating of him as he is in himself in his own rights,
Pressing the pulse of the life that has seldom exhibited itself (the great pride of man in himself),
Chanter of Personality, *outlining what is yet to be, I project the history of the Future.*"

These lines define a large section of Whitman's poems: "the projecting of the Future"—the future, that is to say, of the Ideal Democracy, as well as of the Ideal Man who is to form it.

Those poems which are devoted to this subject are necessarily the least interesting of all Whitman's work to English readers: there is a narrowness of aim in them; they only appeal to the units of a Republic—they chant too exclusively the chants of America. It was, however, with his whole soul that Whitman "projected the history" of America's future, and described his

Stones from a Glass House

ideal of what each man and woman was to be. He sings of a giant race: great men and women, living much in the open, far from what he calls a "puny and pious existence." No doubt he dreams a splendid dream, but whether it is one that is likely to be fulfilled is a question for American prophets to answer.

To our English ideas all Whitman's Democratic ideals are wanting in "atmosphere." We have so steeped ourselves in the traditions of the past that any theory of either Art or Life which ignores these seems bleak to us—wanting in what painters call "atmosphere." We cannot give a whole-hearted admiration here. The past—its great things, its illustrious names, its world-old stories—seems to us far more sacred than the tawdry present. We worship our past; and always will—while America worships her future.

And now we come to a new section of

Walt Whitman

the Whitman poems, and one which marks a distinct era in our author's mental development. At the outbreak of the war Whitman volunteered as a sort of amateur nurse; his experiences in this capacity are embodied in *Drum Taps*. When he deals with " the red business," as he calls it, no one can be finer than Whitman · something of the confusion and terror and roughness of warfare hurtles through his pages—something too of the pity of it— the thrill and the splendour. There drops away from his work now almost all that was objectionable before, sensual-seeming or blatant, and a new note sounds through it. This changed note is infinitely touching when we understand the meaning of it. Three years of toil in the field hospitals had broken down Whitman's strength, and in the prime of life he found himself hopelessly shattered in health. One little disheartened song tells us a whole piteous story of per-

Stones from a Glass House

sonal suffering, if we read between the lines :—

> " Year that trembled and reeled beneath me,
> Your summer wind was warm enough, yet the air I breathed froze me,
> A thick gloom fell through the sunshine and darkened me,
> *' Must I change my triumphant songs ?'* I said to myself,
> 'Must I indeed learn to chant the cold dirges of the baffled and sullen hymns of defeat ?' "

Some premonition of the dark future surely ran through this poem, which seems to have been written at the close of the war, and after Whitman's first serious illness. And henceforward "the triumphant songs" are indeed changed : a spirit of gentleness, humility, resignation, and yet of steady hopefulness and serenity breathes through the verses. They are not the " hymns of defeat," but of victory.

Walt Whitman

Between the years 1873 to 1875 Whitman's life was often despaired of. He hung between life and death, but at last made a partial recovery. "It was said by one of his friends" (says Dr. Maurice Bucke in his Life of Whitman) "that in that combination of illness, poverty, and old age, Whitman has been more grand than in the full vigour of his manhood. For along with illness, pain, and the burden of age, he soon had to bear poverty also. A little while after he became incapacitated by illness he was discharged from his Government clerkship, and everything like an income entirely ceased. As to the profits of *Leaves of Grass* they had never been much, and now two men in succession, in whose hands the sale of the book on commission had been placed, took advantage of his helplessness to embezzle the amounts due, so that, although I hardly ever heard him speak of them, I know that

Stones from a Glass House

during these four years Walt Whitman had to bear the imminent prospect of death, great pain at times, poverty, his poetic enterprise a failure, and the face of the public either clouded in contempt or turned away with indifference. If a man can go through such a trial as this without despair or misanthropy, if he can maintain a good heart, can preserve absolute self-respect, and as absolutely the respect, love, and admiration of the few who thoroughly know him—then he has given proofs, I should say, of personal heroism of the first order It was perhaps needed that Walt Whitman should afford such proofs: at all events he afforded them."

Such a testimony as this is scarcely needed by those who read the last sections of *Leaves of Grass* attentively. The author has so evidently come out on to a higher plane of feeling; the whole conception of things is spiritualised. Under

Walt Whitman

the transparent disguise of a " Prayer of Columbus," we have really the prayer of Walt Whitman—sent up to heaven in his age and weakness, a grander utterance far than the songs of his lusty youth :—

> "One effort more, my altar this bleak sand;
> That Thou, O God, my life hast lighted
> With ray of light, steady, ineffable,
>   vouchsafed by Thee.
>   For that, O God, be it my latest word, here on my knees,
> Old, poor, and paralysed, I thank Thee.
>
> My terminus near,
> The clouds already closing in upon me,
> The voyage balked, the course disputed, lost,
> I yield my ships to Thee.
>
> My hands, my limbs grow nerveless,
> My brain feels racked, bewildered;
> Let the old timbers part, I will not part,

Stones from a Glass House

I will cling fast to Thee, O God,
  though the waves buffet me,
Thee, Thee at least I know.

And these things I see suddenly; what
  mean they?
As if some miracle, some hand divine
  unsealed my eyes;
Shadowy, vast shapes smile through the
  air and sky,
And on the distant waves sail countless
  ships,
And anthems in new tongues I hear
  saluting me!"

Those who make a great profession of any faith are often put to the proof, and it seemed as if after Whitman's arrogant profession of optimism he was to be tested by the most searching of all tests—that of bodily pain and weakness. Long years ago, in the heyday of youth and strength, he made the boast :—

Walt Whitman

"*My foothold is tenon'd and mortis'd in granite,
I laugh at what you call dissolution,*
And I know the amplitude of time."

Now, the world-old history of Job is re-enacted, and we seem once more to hear the Adversary saying, "Skin for skin, yea, all that a man hath will he give for his life; but put forth Thine hand now and touch his bone and his flesh and he will curse Thee to Thy face." But though a new note of dejection—the inevitable result of lessened vitality—is heard every here and there in Whitman's later verse, his old faith in the ultimate good remains unwavering.

Very touching are these verses that speak of the sojourn in Doubting Castle; for example, "*Yet, yet, ye downcast hours.*" These and other random lines tell their own story. Always the idea of "defeat" appears and reappears, as if Whitman's

Stones from a Glass House

whole conception of life was of a great struggle in which he had been worsted. Yet even in this the old optimism triumphs, and he asserts:—

" Did we think victory great?
So it is; *but now it seems to me, when it cannot be helped, that defeat is great*,
And death and dismay are great."

Old and ill and poor and unpopular, with the ideas which he had thought to convert the whole American nation with made into a matter for ridicule, Whitman, though he seems to own himself "defeated" in his life's purpose, still clings to his belief that everything is well-ordered and sure.

"I do not doubt," he says, "that whatever can possibly happen anywhere at any time, is provided for in the inherence of things.

"I do not think that Life provides for all and for Time and Space, but I believe Heavenly Death provides for all."

Walt Whitman

So the old boast made in his strength was tested in his weakness. He laughed at dissolution, for it meant to him not the end, the breaking up of life, but the brave answer to every question, the ultimate victory:—

> "Come, lovely and soothing death,
> Undulate round the world, serenely arriving, arriving,
> In the day, in the night, to all, to each,
> Sooner or later, delicate death.
>
> Praised be the fathomless universe,
> For life, for joy, and for objects and knowledge curious,
> And for love, sweet love—but praise! praise! praise!
> For the sure encircling arms of cool enfolding death.
>
> Dark mother, always gliding near with soft feet,
> Have none chanted for thee a chant of fullest welcome?

Stones from a Glass House

Then I chant it for thee—I glorify thee above all,
I bring thee a song that when those must indeed come, come unfalteringly.

Approach, strong deliveress,
When it is so—when thou hast taken them I joyously sing the dead,
Lost in the loving floating ocean of thee,
Laved in the flood of thy bliss, O death."

Thus Whitman " died and was buried," but his poems remain—a strange memorial of a strange personality.

BY THE SAME AUTHOR

The Story of a Mother

Large Crown 8vo.

2s. 6d.

"A literary achievement which should further advance the name and fame of the gifted authoress of 'The Green Graves of Balgowrie.'"—*Dundee Courier*.

"'The Story of a Mother' is in quite the first rank of the domestic novel."—*Glasgow Herald*.

"Mrs. Jane Findlater may be congratulated upon a tale of great and pathetic beauty."—*Daily Mail*.

"This story has all the charm of truth and freshness . . . the characters are all admirably sketched and endowed with distinct individuality."—*Liverpool Mercury*.

LONDON
JAMES NISBET & CO., LIMITED
21 BERNERS STREET

Letters of
Emelia Russell Gurney

(Mrs. Russell Gurney)

EDITED BY HER NIECE

With Portraits in Photogravure.

Demy 8vo.   12s. 6d.

"The most delightful reading.   It is impossible to speak too highly of these letters, or of the beautiful life and character which they display."—*Speaker*.

"We cannot too warmly recommend this book."—*Spectator*.

"It is positively refreshing to alight unexpectedly upon a book composed of letters of genuine interest."—*Christian World*.

LONDON
JAMES NISBET & CO., LIMITED
21 BERNERS STREET

University of California
SOUTHERN REGIONAL LIBRARY FACILITY
305 De Neve Drive - Parking Lot 17 • Box 951388
LOS ANGELES, CALIFORNIA 90095-1388

Return this material to the library from which it was borrowed.

Lightning Source UK Ltd.
Milton Keynes UK
UKOW06f1826240116

267026UK00007B/214/P